Ghosts of Portsmouth, New Hampshire

Renee Mallett

Schiffer Publishing Ltd®

4880 Lower Valley Road, Atglen, Pennsylvania 19310

Schiffer Books are available at special discounts for bulk purchases for sales promotions or premiums. Special editions, including personalized covers, corporate imprints, and excerpts can be created in large quantities for special needs. For more information contact the publisher:

Published by Schiffer Publishing Ltd.
4880 Lower Valley Road
Atglen, PA 19310
Phone: (610) 593-1777; Fax: (610) 593-2002
E-mail: Info@schifferbooks.com

Please visit our web site catalog at www.schifferbooks.com

We are always looking for people to write books on new and related subjects. If you have an idea for a book, please contact us at the above address.

This book may be purchased from the publisher. Include $5.00 for shipping.
Please try your bookstore first. You may write for a free catalog.

In Europe, Schiffer books are distributed by:
Bushwood Books
6 Marksbury Ave.
Kew Gardens
Surrey TW9 4JF
England
Phone: 44 (0)208 392-8585
Fax: 44 (0)208 392-9876
E-mail: Info@bushwoodbooks.co.uk

Website: www.bushwoodbooks.co.uk
Free postage in the UK. Europe: air mail at cost.
Try your bookstore first.

Designed by Stephanie Daugherty
Type set in A Charming Font Expanded/NewBskvll BT

ISBN: 978-0-7643-3161-9
Printed in the United States of America

Dedication

This book is dedicated to my family, for their love and support. None of my books could have been written without them.

Acknowledgements

This is my third book with Schiffer Publishing, and the second book on haunted places I've done with them. The first book was Manchester Ghosts and the success of that book, and the plain old good time I had writing it, was a great motivator and inspiration for writing this book, Ghosts of Portsmouth, New Hampshire. I'd like to thank everyone who helped make the creation and publication of Manchester Ghosts the wonderful experience it was. So, thanks to Dinah Roseberry, who is the best editor any writer could ask for, Joe Langman and the rest of the publicity and marketing team, and everyone else at Schiffer Books who has made the publishing experience such a treat for me.

I'd also like to thank Claire Berwick, along with the rest of the staff at the Barnes and Noble in Manchester New Hampshire, for their support throughout my writing career. As I said in Manchester Ghosts, it's not what you know, it's who you know, and I'm very lucky to know this group of dedicated booksellers.

I am greatly indebted, too, to the wonderful staff of the Chester Public Library, and especially the head librarian Melissa Rossetti, for always managing to find the book I need (and overlooking just how long I tend to keep that book once they find it for me).

Contents

Author's Note

This is a book of real-life ghost stories and other paranormal or otherwise unexplainable occurrences. The stories are based on first-person accounts, and some of the cases are quite famous and have been reported both online and in other books or magazines as well. Many of the stories, like all great ghost stories, have an element of local legend or folklore to them, and they walk the thin line between fiction and fact.

This book would not exist without the generosity of the people who have decided to shared their experiences and, as the old saying goes, many of the names have been changed to protect the identity of the people involved.

Please keep in mind that all of the places written about in this book are real places that offer you, the reader, the opportunity to go and visit yourself. That being said, all of these places are private residences, and places of business or education. Before visiting any haunted site, remember that the living people in these places deserve respect and privacy first and foremost. Exact house numbers and street names are not given for any of the private homes in this book. Never trespass on other peoples property; always get permission before you decide to go ghost hunting and decide to visit a haunted site. All ghost hunters are legally responsible for their own actions.

In Portsmouth, there are a great many companies and tours that make the rounds to haunted sites, especially in the month of October. These ghost tours are an ideal, safe, and legal way to experience haunted places and ghostly phenomena yourself, usually for a modest admission fee and without taking on the added risk of a trespassing charge.

Introduction

Welcome to Portsmouth, New Hampshire: A Haunted Travel Destination

Portsmouth, New Hampshire, despite having a population of only a little more than 20,000 people, is a popular tourist destination that draws visitors from all over the country. The National Trust for Historic Preservation has named Portsmouth one of its "Dozen Distinctive Destinations." It describes the city as "one of the most culturally rich destinations in the country with a stimulating mix of historic buildings, sidewalk cafes, great restaurants, jazz clubs, and distinctive artisans boutiques." The only thing they forgot to mention was the ghosts!

On top of being a cultural hotspot, Portsmouth also happens to be one of the most haunted cities in New England—if not the entire country. Outside of Salem, Massachusetts, it is considered to be New England's premier paranormal vacation spot. And, much like their witch-burning neighbors to the south, Portsmouth doesn't try to hide their spooks. Instead, Portsmouth revels in its more unusual tourist attractions. It is no exaggeration to say that ghosts have become big business in this small ocean-front community. Shop keepers are quick to tell about their encounters with resident ghosts and there are several walking tours that show visitors where the spectral hot spots are while giving them a lesson in some of Portsmouth's shadier history. Every October, more and more ghostly tours pop up and tourists have their pick of wandering through the historic homes of Strawbery Banke and learning about their ghosts, taking a walking tour and learning about the spectral side of Portsmouth's history, or even bar hopping with the help of one of the city's resident pub ghost experts!

Part of what makes Portsmouth such an interesting place is that it is a small city that has a big history. It is one of the oldest remaining cities that survive from the original thirteen colonies that made up the young United States. Notable Portsmouth residents through the ages include several United States representatives, a handful of Generals and Governors, the famed socialite and philanthropist Brooke Astor, famed musicians Ronnie James Dio and Tom Rush, an astronaut, one of the signers of the Declaration of Independence, the "father of the United States Navy" John Paul Jones, and Betty and Barney Hill, who rose to fame in the 1960s after they became the victims of the first widely reported alien abduction in the U.S. (and about whom you can read more about in a later chapter in this book). Some of these famous residents seem to have liked Portsmouth so much they've decided to linger on—even after death!

Portsmouth is a wonderful mix of the old and new; it is a city that has all the options and attractions of a major metropolitan city, with the friendliness of a small town. When visiting the city, it is impossible to ignore how old it actually is, as many of its buildings, dating from the 1800s and long before, are still standing and have been carefully restored to their former glory. And, if somehow you start to overlook the incredible age of the city, its history has a way of popping back up at unexpected moments.

In 2004, a road crew, working in the middle of downtown Portsmouth's busiest intersection was surprised when a backhoe struck a heavy wooden object deep below ground. They almost couldn't believe it when they realized they had just dug up a very, very old coffin! And, even more surprisingly, this coffin wasn't the only one they dug up that day. They ended up with several eighteenth-century coffins under the city street, which held the remains of thirteen

Street-side crypts in Portsmouth's downtown area. You wouldn't believe what you might find under the street!

different people. Although the bodies were severely deteriorated after more than 200 years under ground, DNA testing confirmed the suspicions of several town historians. The remains were those of African slaves. Early Portsmouth records had shown the existence of a segregated cemetery, which at that time was at the far outskirts of the city. As the town grew, many old cemeteries were moved and shuffled around through the ages. But the exact location of the segregated graveyard had gotten lost in the shuffle. Today no one is sure exactly how the bodies came to be left behind, or overlooked, as the city expanded.

Is it possible that the town fathers, in the late 1700s, would have allowed buildings and streets to spring up right on top of consecrated ground without moving the bodies? Could these bodies have been accidentally buried outside the cemetery land and unmarked so no one knew to move them? Like much of history, there is a lot of speculation, but no easy answers. Because the bodies all belonged to young adults, and one to a relatively small child, there has been some speculation about a much darker scenario that resulted in them being buried unbeknownst to the city fathers. Perhaps these were slaves that were killed by their owners and buried in unmarked graves. They may have even been killed as a punishment for trying to escape. It is likely that we will never know how these people came to be buried here.

Many archaeologists who have visited the site seem convinced that, like a scene straight out of the movie *Poltergeist*, there are many more undiscovered bodies waiting to be found under the streets and homes of Portsmouth. Unbelievable as it seems, many historians have said that they believe there are as many as an additional 200 bodies deep below the city.

The more we learn of Portsmouth's history, the more questions are answered about the city's ghostly inhabitants. While there are certainly plenty of modern-day haunts to be found in Portsmouth, New Hampshire, its true charm is in the historical hauntings that make this a unique and unparalleled destination for those looking for a close encounter with the things that go bump in the night.

The Haunted Library

The Old Portsmouth Public Library Building on Islington Street

Itt seems as though spirits are drawn to libraries, and the Portsmouth Public library, located downtown in Islington Street proves the rule. There have been reports of a good half a dozen different ghosts that have taken up residence among the stacks. Most seem to be quiet spirits, ones who interact little to never with the living, but the library has a few more spirited ghosts that are well known to Portsmouth's book lovers.

Standing in the reference room, if you look up onto the overhead balcony, you may catch a glimpse of a curly-headed child walking along the railings. Blink and the child is gone. Like many of the library's ghosts, no one is sure where this one came from but he or she (as there are conflicting reports on the ghosts gender) has been seen quite often and can appear anywhere on the upper floor. The spirit is usually only visible when standing at the railing, but the sound of a child running is heard throughout the balcony. Some library visitors also hear a child playing, or shuffling through old books, in the aisle next to theirs. When they go to ask the child where their parent is, the aisle is empty, though sometimes the shadow of the child will be seen on the floor—even with no person there to cast it! This child-like ghost has even been accused of stacking books neatly along the floor, just like the librarian ghost seen in the movie Ghostbusters.

The polar opposite of the playful little child is the ghost of a stern librarian who has taken up residence in the Special Collections room at the Portsmouth Public Library building. This room houses all of the library's books on the history of Portsmouth, a collection of art by Portsmouth residents, and the ghost of a grumpy old librarian. Most people only report an eerie feeling while browsing the books in the Special Collections room, or walking into cold spots, but a few more rambunctious patrons have been severely shushed by the stern old librarian that can't see. If the hush doesn't manage to get readers under control, a few pinches by the unseen something almost always does the trick.

While the other ghosts seem to be ones who have stayed on from a long ago past, there is one often-seen spirit, dressed in modern-day clothing, who wanders Islington Street outside the library building

The front entrance way to the Portsmouth Public Library on Islington Street.

This, the 'old' Portsmouth Public Library, has since been replaced by a more energy efficient building located on Parrott Avenue.

and sometimes pops in for a bit. This ghostly man walks throughout the library, unmindful of the walls and closed doors that he simply passes through without noticing, and after awhile, he walks back out onto Islington Street.

The Portsmouth Public Library on Islington Street is currently sitting empty . . . of any living readers at least! Just before the dawn of 2007, the construction of a brand new, spacious, energy-efficient public library was completed and the city's treasure trove of books was moved to this new location. Since then, the building on Islington Street has become known as the "Old Portsmouth Library," and debate has raged about what, exactly, should be done with it. The cumbersome building, actually three buildings from varied time periods combined into one unwieldy beast, has an estimated value that some say could be as much as a million dollars. The quick sale of the old building could certainly help the city of Portsmouth offset some of the costs incurred by the construction of the new library.

There was a strong push to turn the building into a visitor's welcome center and that has come to fruition. With Portsmouth seeing larger and larger influxes of tourists each year, there was certainly a need for such a place. One can't help but think that this option is what the old Portsmouth Public Library's ghostly inhabitants would prefer.

Point of Graves

The Strange Glow Around Vaughan's Tomb
and Other Strange Happenings in This Seventeenth-Century Cemetery

This plaque educates visitors about the more unusual grave markers and the final resting places of some of Point of Graves more illustrious residents. It makes no mention of the cemetery's famous ghosts.

stablished in the late 1600s, upon a bequeath of land to the town from Captain John Pickering, Point of Graves Burial Ground is the oldest cemetery in the city of Portsmouth. The oldest gravestone in the cemetery, at least the oldest that is currently both standing and legible enough to read, dates all the way back to 1682. None of the earlier gravestones seem to have survived— most likely because Captain Pickering encouraged his cows to graze among the stones long after he himself gave the city the land to use as a burial site! Historians believe that the Pickering family used this half-acre plot of land for a burial ground long before giving it to the city for public use, so no one knows just how old this cemetery may really be or even how many bodies are buried there.

Today, the cemetery is surprisingly well maintained given its age, and is now free from the destructive nature of hungry clumsy bovine. It features many notable tombstones, especially from the Colonial era, that draw gravestone rubbers from all over New England. In Point of Graves Burial Ground, you can see many fine examples of tombstone work from the Massachusetts artists William Mumford and John Homer, among others. Many prominent figures from New Hampshire's history have been buried in this cemetery. But, even though it is the final resting place of captains, Lieutenants, and Governors, all memorialized by beautifully hand-carved tombstones, many visitors to Point of Graves are drawn here, not to browse the headstones, but to see if they can experience some of the otherworldly things that are rumored to go one here.

Near the 1717 grave of Elizabeth Pierce, some visitors have felt a small shove back towards the grave as they walk away. It's as if the woman buried there doesn't want to be left alone. Others have reported feeling of something tugging at their clothes or even an icy grip clutching at their arms and hands. The sensations only come as people try to leave the area around Elizabeth Pierce's grave and never as they walk towards it.

Oftentimes, visitors to Point of Graves come out convinced they were being followed by something they couldn't see. The eerie sound of a man's heavy footsteps seems to plague visitors who have the bad luck to come to the cemetery when no one else is around.

One young mother who had brought her children with her to see the gravestones, said that the footsteps seemed to follow her children very closely, and lingered around two small graves bearing the young ages of children that had died in the early 1800s of yellow fever. Could this be evidence of a ghostly father searching for his children among the graves? Some particularly sensitive people think exactly that; they have also picked up on a sense of mourning lingering around this part of the cemetery. A few have even reported seeing the shadowy figure of a crying man bent over the two small gravestones like a parent grieving for his deceased children.

More disturbingly are the people who come with a camera and walk away with some uncanny pictures as a souvenir of their visit. The Vaughan tomb, in particular, though no ghosts have been seen or sensed there, sometimes appears in photographs surrounded by strange, wildly-colored lights, or emitting a peculiar greenish-yellow glow. To date, no one has been able to come up with a sound scientific

Grave stone rubbers and cemetery enthusiasts come from all over New England to see the beautifully carved tombstones that grace Point of Graves Cemetery.

While not as unusually decorated as some of the other grave markers in this cemetery, the simple clean lines of the Vaughan tomb are probably the most photographed, by both paranormal investigators, skeptics, and the curious.

reason for the strange aura that encompasses this gravestone. Skeptics have passed the glow off as the reflection of the street light on the smooth white stone of the crypt, but the glow is visible no matter which angle or side of the grave you view. Even more convincingly, it is the only grave to glow in such a way. If it truly was just the reflection of an outside light source, wouldn't the graves surrounding it glow as well?

In the most unusual occurrence happening at Point of Graves Burial Ground, a ghostly walking tour, accompanied by a reporter who later published an article on the strange phenomena, got more than just a quick haunted history lesson. As the day deepened into evening and the sky tuned black, the clouds above the cemetery were said to roil and turn wispy pink. Fifteen witnesses all agreed that the clouds clearly formed the bodies and wings of angels.

The John Paul Jones House and Museum

Love and Loss From Beyond the Veil at the John Paul Jones House
Located at the Corner of Middle and State Streets

J ohn Paul Jones is one of those larger-than-life figures of whom stories abound even long after they die. Of course, John Paul Jones is rumored to be living on past death, too. And, if there's any truth behind a rumor more than 200 years old, there's a good chance that the kindly widow who loved him in life has stayed by his side even in death.

The John Paul Jones House and Museum, located at the corner of Middle Street and State Street, is also the home of Portsmouth's Historical Society.

The Portsmouth Historical Society resides in a lovingly restored yellow Georgian-style home dating from 1758 that is known as the John Paul Jones House. This is something of a misnomer. While John Paul Jones did live in the home for several years, he was never anything more than a boarder there. The house began as a wedding gift to Sarah Wentworth Purcell from her new husband, Gregory, a prosperous sea captain. The couple had thirteen children, at least half of whom survived the dangerous infant years. Unfortunately, this story doesn't have a happy ending to match its auspicious beginning. Gregory Purcell died, probably from a long drawn-out illness contracted while at sea. Purcell left his widow, Sarah, with a great big debt, a very limited inheritance, and even less options about how to solve the first two problems. In order to make ends meet, Sarah Purcell turned the stately home into a boarding house. Thus enters John Paul Jones.

John Paul Jones was the Revolutionary war hero who was credited as being the father of the American Navy. During the fight for the American colony's independence from England, he is reputed to have refused a British officer's call to surrender, replying rather famously, "I have not yet begun to fight!" It was in the late 1770s that John Paul Jones started spending a lot of time in Portsmouth and took up residence at Sarah Purcell's rooming house, undoubtedly never imagining that the very same home would bear his name hundreds of years later.

While John Paul Jones only lived as a boarder in this Georgian style home, his ghost continues to walk its hallways, perhaps searching for the woman he loved in life.

While Sarah Purcell was a widow of some standing, owning one of the most elegant homes in Portsmouth at the time, tongues always wagged a bit over her relationship with the legendary naval hero. Perhaps it was simply idle talk, or maybe there was some truth behind the stories. No one really knows for sure and it is unlikely at this point that we'll ever know definitively if she and John Paul Jones had a strict tenant-landlord relationship, or were lovers.

A year after John Paul Jones left Portsmouth, Sarah Purcell sold the gabled Georgian to her next door neighbor, Woodbury Langdon. After that time, the house passed hands quickly through dozens of different owners, and was rented, leased, and renovated almost as often. The house has been called home by a Portsmouth Postmaster, a U.S. Senator, and many prominent Portsmouth businessmen. Sadly, in later years, the house went through a steady period of decline, came close to being demolished a few times, was turned into a turn-of-the-century office building, then a tea room, and, perhaps, a hotel. In 1917, it was bought by Cappy Stewart, a man who made his fortune owning and running brothels in Portsmouth's tawdry red-light district, until the city shut him down in 1915. Cappy planned on tearing the house down and public opinion turned even more against him than it had when he was simply known as the owner of houses of ill repute. Editorials were written in the local paper, citizens decried losing the place John Paul Jones once lived, and former business associates cut him dead on the streets.

In a surprising twist of fate, in walked another Woodbury Langdon, who just happened to be the namesake and great grandson of the man who had bought the property from Sarah Purcell originally. In a behind-the-scenes deal, he took the home and grounds off the hands of Cappy Stewart for an unspecified sum, and then formed the Portsmouth Historical Society to watch over the home.

In an outpouring of generosity, the populace of Portsmouth raided their attics and storage rooms and gave freely of their family heirlooms to the newly formed Historic Society. The John Paul Jones House still has these items on display. After hundreds of years of dishevel the house has settled back down into a routine, and it has been restored to the same shape it was in during its heyday. By the time the house was redone and the historical society was ready to open its doors to the public, the ghost stories had already begun to spread.

On the days when the building is closed to visitors, and no Historical Society people are scheduled to be at work, people passing by still see the figure of a woman walking from room to room.

Sometimes this white-faced specter pulls aside the curtains and gazes out the window as though she is oblivious to the cars coming by on State Street and is waiting for someone to walk up the street. She is said to have a look of longing on her face and carries a sad air around her.

Inside the museum, most often in the so called "shawl room," cabinet doors open and shut on their own while guides are trying to give tours. During lunch breaks, many workers have heard the distinctive sound of the back door opening and closing even when they know they are the only people in the building. Enough people at John Paul Jones House have had the feeling that they were not alone in a room, even when they could see very well that they were, that professional ghost hunters from Pennsylvania came on scene to see whether they could find more concrete evidence of a haunting. With the pale-faced lady ghost seen so often from the street, is seemed a foregone conclusion that this team would say they had "discovered" the ghost of Sarah Purcell. What the men came back with, instead, was some evidence of a male figure hovering in and around the very same dressing room and bedroom that had been rented to John Paul Jones so many years before.

While we can never be sure who the ghosts of John Paul Jones House actually are, it's hard to dispel the romantic notion of John and Sarah reuniting from beyond the veil.

The Gourmet Ghost

The Residential Home With an Unseen Chef Stirring the Pot

Marybeth doesn't consider her house a haunted one in the traditional sense, though she does admit that at least one spirit occupies the chefs' apron in her kitchen. This gourmet ghost helps her pick her recipes, find needed kitchen utensils, and even—Marybeth is just sure of it—adds just the right spices and herbs to flavor her meals.

Marybeth isn't sure who her ghost is, or where it came from. She doesn't live in an old building, or one with a notable history. She'd lived uneventfully in the house for years before the spirit ever made its presence known. But boy, when it decided to make itself known, it did so with a bang—literally!

It was a typical morning in a typical quiet residential Portsmouth neighborhood. Marybeth was making herself some eggs for breakfast. She placed the spatula carefully on the counter and turned away, walking towards the refrigerator to pour herself a glass of orange juice. As she reached for the door handle, she felt as though someone had just walked into the kitchen with her. She turned just in time to see the spatula lift itself up off the counter and fling itself across the room, flipping end over end. Marybeth stood frozen as the utensil clattered noisily to the floor.

Hesitantly, Marybeth walked over to where the spatula laid, still now, on the yellow linoleum. As she bent over to pick it up, a thousand different scenarios played themselves out in her mind, but no matter how wild of an idea she came up with, she couldn't imagine what had caused the spatula to fly across the room like that. Her orange juice forgotten, Marybeth placed the spatula carefully up on the counter again, taking care that it was not near the hot stove or the edge of the countertop. It lay there dully. The housewife, and mother of four, began to think that maybe she had imagined the whole thing. Sighing with relief, she went back to the fridge to get something to drink.

When she turned around again, the spatula had moved itself from the counter top into the sink.

Marybeth closed her eyes and counted to ten, slowly. When she opened them, the spatula was still there. Then, right before her eyes, the sink faucet turned by an unseen hand and water poured from the tap. She couldn't help but feel as if someone was gently chiding her for not washing the spatula after it had touched the floor.

Despite this abrupt and startling beginning, Marybeth and her ghost soon became friends, joined by a love of cooking. Some days, she finds her cook books open on the counter and Marybeth always takes this as a suggestion of what she should cook for supper that night. She says she has discovered some great recipes that way. If, while cooking, Marybeth loses track of an ingredient or utensil she needs, all she has to do is politely ask her ghost if he knows where it is and, more often than not, when she turns around she finds the item sitting in the middle of the counter in plain sight. Several times, when tasting a meal she herself just cooked, Marybeth detects the flavor of some spice or herb she knows she never included in the recipe. All she can figure is that her unseen sous chef decided to improve on her cooking.

They say that too many cooks spoil the broth, but Marybeth doesn't agree. Her ghostly gourmet is considered a part of the family and he hasn't turned out a bad meal yet.

The Parsonage

An Office Building on State Street

This building, located on State Street, was built in 1749, and was originally used as a parsonage. The church that was located next door is now long gone and the parsonage itself has since been turned into offices. Interestingly, this building is also linked to the subterranean maze of tunnels beneath Portsmouth's streets that may have been part of the Underground Railroad.

Some unusual spirits haunt this office building, especially considering it was, for many years, the home of members of the clergy. Most of the manifestations in this building run the spectrum from terribly unhappy to surprisingly angry. Workers are often disturbed at their desks when they feel a melancholy presence standing at their backs. The weeping spirit is usually invisible to the human eye but a rare few report seeing a vague gray mist where the crying originates.

This sad specter is in sharp contrast to the belligerent ghost that stomps angrily up the back stairwell and slams doors throughout the building. This spirit seems to come and go. Weeks or months will go by without a peep from it, but when the ghost decides to make itself known, it really goes all out. When the angry spirit's haunting is at its peak, sometimes items are seem being tossed across the office by unseen hands. This ghost even seems to affect the behavior of the people within the office itself. Workers say they are more irritable and stressed out when this spirit is at its worst.

The Rockingham Hotel

A Former Hotel Turned Condominiums Located on State Street

The Rockingham Hotel is located on the exact site of a former mansion that was built by Woodbury Langdon in 1785. By 1833, the beautiful estate had been converted into one of New England's premier hotels. Less than fifty years later, this hotel would become the property of Frank Jones, Portsmouth's celebrated brewer and an owner of several fine hotels.

In 1884, disaster struck the hotel. The building that had managed to survive Portsmouth's Great Fire of 1813 was completely decimated in a much smaller blaze. When the smoke cleared, all that remained of the famous hotel was its dining room. Frank Jones, however, was not daunted by this turn of ill fortune. Sparing no expense, he had an entire new hotel built up around the remaining dining room. News reports at the time tell us that the overall budget for this project surpassed that of the amount it cost to build the Portsmouth Naval Shipyard.

The Rockingham Hotel opened to much fanfare. Over the years, Presidents Franklin Pierce, James Polk, William Taft, John F. Kennedy, and Theodore Roosevelt have all stayed at the hotel. Everything from its lighting fixtures to its ceiling were crafted by the most well-respected and skilled craftsmen of the time.

More unusual additions to the hotel were not as talked about. Frank Jones had a series of underground tunnels built from his various properties and businesses around the city, all congregating under the hotel's bottom floor. These tunnels may have been an expansion of tunnels already existing under the city, possibly as part of the Underground Railroad, but Jones used them to transport his popular liquor from one building to another. In modern day, very few of the tunnels have been explored or researched and it is said that all the tunnels under and around the Rockingham Hotel have collapsed or been filled in.

In 1973, the Rockingham Hotel began its new life as a condominium complex and a few years later, a restaurant opened in its downstairs. It was not long after this that the talk of ghosts started up. One ghost has been seen quite often walking from the Rockingham Hotel to the John Paul Jones House which is owned by the Portsmouth Historical Society. When it arrives at the well-

The Rockingham Hotel has been home to a United States Senator, Portsmouth's most famous brewer, a brothel owner, a woman thought to be the mistress of John Paul Jones, Portsmouth's Poet Laureate and several ghosts.

maintained yellow Georgian home, it walks around the first floor peering into the windows.

It has long been thought that the wife of Woodbury Langdon had an affair with John Paul Jones when he stayed in Portsmouth. The ghostly woman seems to give some evidence to the rumor that was talked about enough during its time that it remains a subject of gossip today. Considering that John Paul Jones has also been linked to his landlady, Sarah Wentworth Purcell, one can't help but wonder if Mrs. Langdon is trying to catch John Paul being unfaithful to her.

Esther Buffler, elected Portsmouth's first Poet Laureate in 1998, was also a resident of the Rockingham Hotel. She became famous for a poem about her experiences with one of the Rockingham Hotel's ghosts. Soon after moving into the condominium, Esther was visited by a ghost sheathed in a white dress. This spirit had a calming presence and, Esther asserted, smelled strongly of the ocean.

Others too have encountered the rogue scent of the briny sea, though very few are sensitive enough to physically see the spirit as Esther Buffler was. All agree that there is nothing frightening about this spirit. Calming is the word most often associated with this ghost, though tranquil and serene get mentioned nearly as often. The ghost's placid nature has caused some debate about who this spirit actually belongs to. It is well documented that, when the Rockingham Hotel was still a hotel, a young woman who was staying there as a guest accidentally drowned while swimming in the Atlantic.

It seems likely that a spirit smelling of the sea would belong to the young lady who met her untimely death in the ocean, but shouldn't the ghost seem more frantic? Ghosts linked to accidental deaths are not normally known for their serenity and there is no reason anyone has unearthed why the young woman's spirit would be roaming the hallways of the hotel where she stayed rather than at the site of her actual demise.

Wine and Spirits

Bars and Pubs With a Fine History of Haunting

The Portsmouth of today is a popular destination for tourists and locals alike who want to go out on the town. No surprise there; the city has always been known for its nightlife. In the 1800s, Portsmouth had only 6,000 residents and close to 200 bars! Of course, don't forget that Portsmouth was always a harbor town. That 6,000 only includes the permanent residents, and doesn't even begin to touch on the ten to fifteen thousand sailors that visited the city weekly during the nineteenth century. And along with the bars came the brothels, fights, murders, and more. Portsmouth holds the record for having more unsolved murders than any other town in the state. But before you get the idea that it's a city overridden with crime, bear in mind that the clear bulk of those crimes took place in the 1800s. Portsmouth today is actually one of the safest towns you can imagine with crime levels all well below the national averages.

But some of these brawling drunken pub lovers liked the time they spent in Portsmouth so much they've decided to stay on, and keep on visiting their favorite taverns. Here are just a few of the many establishments in Portsmouth that offer wine and spirits.

Molly Malone's

Molly Malone's is an old school Irish pub and a popular Portsmouth hangout. It is as well known for its much-publicized ghosts as it is for its inviting atmosphere and friendly staff. It is housed in a brick building on State Street that dates back to 1815. Before it was a bar, it was a boarding house and, if you had the money to spend, the second floor rooms came with a girl to keep you company. This building was actually only one of an estimated forty brothels that were operating in the city at this time and the competition between these businesses created something of a red-light district in this turn-of-the-century neighborhood. Girls would put on their most becoming dresses and lounge in the upstairs windows of the establishments they worked at, calling out come-ons and promises to the men walking by in the hopes of luring them in for a night's entertainment.

Molly Malone's, built in 1815, started life as a hotel and brothel. Today it is a popular Portsmouth night spot that comes complete with ghosts.

Passersby are sometimes surprised to hear cat calls coming from the 'ladies of the night' who have stayed on at Molly Malone's long after death.

Two of these ladies of the night are still hard at work and are sometimes seen by people walking up State Street. Much as they must have a hundred years ago, they still lean from the windows, smiling invitingly as they wave to passersby, and sometimes can faintly be heard urging men to come inside. Their presence is still felt inside the bar as well. It is common to hear feet pounding up and down the back stairwell all night long as though unseen men are still running upstairs to see the ladies, even though when employees go to check on the noises, they find no one there.

These ladies of the night are playful spirits who have been blamed for several pranks in Molly Malone's, like hiding keys, which were in plain view moments before, and locking the bathroom stalls from the inside after closing time. It is a common enough bar-room prank, found in very much non-haunted bars all around the country, but at Molly Malone's, you can be sure they are being perpetrated by phantoms, and not drunks, since the stall doors come close enough to the floor that no living person could squeeze their way underneath in order to lock the door and leave.

The second floor of Molly Malone's, in between its time as a brothel and its current reincarnation as a bar, was once apartments. One tenant of these apartments was found dead of a heart attack when the sheriff came to evict him for non-payment of rent. Since the man had no family and no money of his own, he was buried in an unmarked pauper's grave and his name has been forgotten in the passing years. He seems to still call Molly Malone's home though and is upset at being forgotten. Oftentimes, when workers leave for the night, they see a light switched on in a second floor room after they've already locked up. No one feels like investigating, and possibly coming face to face with a ghost, especially since the lights are always off when they arrive again in the morning. The ghost carries around him the chill of the grave. The second floor of Molly Malone's has trouble with their heat. No matter how many times it is looked at, the thermostat changes itself at a whim, and the heat is always getting cranked up.

Molly Malone's kitchen has a ghost infestation as well. Several cooks and busboys have felt tugs at their hair when no one was standing near them and at least one has seen the volume control on the kitchen radio turned up loud by an unseen hand.

Several workers have seen a man in a white lab coat walking around the basement. When confronted, he disappears through the wall, which is a firmly bricked-over opening that once led to a tunnel. This tunnel may have been part of the Underground Railroad that helped lead escaped slaves to the states in the north that had outlawed slavery in the eighteenth century. Ironically, it may have also been used to lead men into slavery. It has long been rumored that, in times gone by of Portsmouth's busy seaport days, when patrons racked up a bar tab they could not afford to pay off, they were kidnapped and forced into servitude on an oceangoing ship in order to clear their debts. A more mundane explanation for the bricked-over tunnel is that it dates from the 1800s when Frank Jones Brewery on Islington Street was the largest brewery on the East Coast. The tunnels may have been used to safely and efficiently carry alcohol from the brewery, and its warehouses, to the local pubs. It may seem odd, given Molly Malone's colorful history, that the figure seen was wearing a lab coat. But, after so many people reported seeing this figure, it came to light that, for a brief time, the basement had served as an apothecary shop whose owner surely would have worn a white lab coat or something very similar.

The brother of Molly Malone's owner was in the basement once when the lights clicked out. Thinking quickly, he pulled out his camera phone and took pictures blindly in the dark. When the lights came on and he checked his phone, he had captured an image of a yellow mist that looked something like a very small child. Who that child could be is a mystery considering the building's history.

In the bar itself there is at least one ghost who likes patrons to keep things happy. When voices are raised, or if a fight looks imminent, glasses have been seen flying off the bar and sometimes even smashing against the wall with enough force to shatter them. During one such argument, between two owners of the bar, several glasses flew off all at once before smashing into the wall located a good eight feet away from the counter.

Another common occurrence is the ice-cold breezes that waft through the bar as though someone has left a door open . . . even when someone hasn't. Particularly sensitive patrons have even had conversations with other people at the bar they do not recognize as ghosts until the person they've spent the evening chatting with disappears before their very eyes!

The Black Trumpet Bistro

The Black Trumpet is a bistro and wine bar located at 29 Ceres Street. The building at Ceres Street has been home to several of Portsmouth's most award winning and beloved restaurants, the Blue Strawbery and Lindbergh's Crossing among them. The culinary pedigree this building holds in many ways outshines its more unusual history. Originally, the brick and stone building housed a ships' chandlery. Chandleries can be found today; they mostly sell basic ship maintenance supplies and food for the crew, but historically, chandleries were much more than simple retail stores. Not only would ships buy every item they would need for long ocean voyages at a chandlery, but they also depended on the store to act as their liaison with port officials and local governments when docking. Having a good relationship with a decent chandlery could make all the difference in the profitability of a ship's run. The building at Ceres Street was one of the most important chandleries in Portsmouth during the height of its use as a shipping port. It can only be assumed that the most famous, and most infamous, of Portsmouth's residents and visitors passed through this building at one point or another.

Like all great restaurants, and The Black Trumpet Bistro is considered to be one of Portsmouth's most distinguished,

People come to the Black Trumpet Bistro expecting a fine dining experience. Some people get more than they bargained for when they realize a ghostly host walks the dining room.

atmosphere is everything. Happy dinners walk away not only talking about their fabulous meal or great service, but the overall welcoming feel of the building. Many suspect that part of this appeal emanates from the benign spirits that haunt the building, spirits that date from the buildings use as a chandlery.

The haunting at The Black Trumpet Bistro is, by all accounts, more subtle then you'll find at some of the other eateries mentioned here. There is definitely a feeling of not being alone in a room, even when you can see you are, or gentle wafts of sweetly-scented cold spots. Overall, though, most people just walk away from their ghostly run-ins with a sense of something spectral, and a feeling that whatever they have had a run-in with, loves the old building at Ceres Street very much.

AK'S Bar and Bistro

The building that is home to AK's Bar and Bistro has, like Molly Malone's, been many bars, businesses, and brothels in its time. The original building was destroyed in the Great Fire of 1813; the building currently standing at 111 State Street was built on the foundations of the old one in 1814.

For many years it was the site of the Old Bridge Café, a place that was well known to residents and Portsmouth police as one of the roughest bars in town. It made the news several times during its run. When the body of a young woman was found murdered and dumped in Lincoln, New Hampshire, police traced her back all the way to the Old Bridge Café. It was the last place the girl was seen alive, and in the company of some not very nice men. In the fall of 1998, the Old Bridge Café was the scene of a near riot that ended in several people being injured and a police cruiser damaged. Then a year later a man was found stabbed to death outside the bar after a bartender kicked him out.

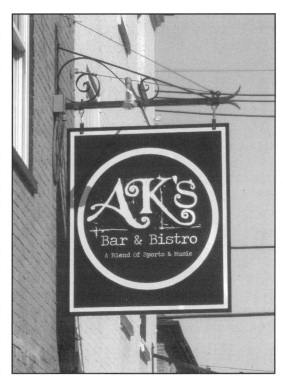

Built around the same time as Molly Malone's AK's Bar and Grill is also known for its ghosts— and a much darker history than you'll find attached to the Irish pub.

Enough was enough. The Old Bridge Café was closed down and later reopened as Jack Quigley's bar. It was around this time that the ghost stories started to circulate. Waitresses refused to go up to the second floor, where the offices were, unaccompanied. They felt what could only be described as a malignant presence on that floor and sometimes a dark mist was seen out of the corner of their eyes as they hurried through. One waitress discounted the ghost stories until the night she was on the second floor and, looking into the long mirror that lined the hallway, saw a man standing right behind her. She whirled around to tell the man they were closed, but found no one there. Not believing her eyes, she looked back into the mirror and saw the vague outline of the man fading into nothing. She hurried from the building and felt pursued until she stepped outside.

The second floor and basement of this 1814 building are paranormal hot spots, even in a town that is known for it's ghostly tourist attractions.

From downstairs, many workers report hearing footsteps pacing the second floor when they know it is unoccupied. One night, several people heard loud scrapes and thumps coming from the second floor. When they went upstairs to see what was making the noise, they found all of the barstools, which had been screwed into the floor, thrown around like a child's toys after a tantrum.

Not all of the ghostly activity is confined to the second floor though. Much like Molly Malone's, the basement at 111 State Street is supposed to be haunted, but their ghost is something much darker than the white-coated apothecary apparition. Darting shapes, random cold spots, and deep booming and dark laughter have all been felt and heard by people sent downstairs to bring up supplies.

Jack Quigley's was beset by more then just problems of a ghostly nature and closed its doors as well. The spot where it once stood is now AK's Bar and Bistro. There's been no word yet from the new owners if the ghosts have stayed on.

Portsmouth Brewery

Portsmouth Brewery is located at 56 Market Street, in the very heart of downtown Portsmouth. They have been a New Hampshire landmark for close to twenty years. At the Portsmouth Brewery, you can get some great pub food, a wonderful handcrafted beer, and possibly a ghostly encounter.

The most haunted room at the Portsmouth Brewery seems to be the Jimmy LaPanza Room. This room is home to a female ghost who

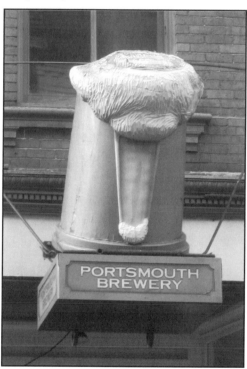

more than one person has described as "sultry." This sultry spirit seems to like to get frisky with patrons, with a teasing goose here or a not so painful pinch there but, so far as anyone is willing to admit, she hasn't been physically seen by anyone. She seems to carry a sizzling aura around with her that even those without the slightest hint of psychic ability can pick up on.

The history of this provocative lady is a mystery. There are those who claim that she is the woman depicted in a mural in the Portsmouth Brewery. There are those who claim she is a girlfriend, mistress, or simply someone who had a crush on Jimmy LaPanza himself.

The Portsmouth Brewery is a treat for anyone who loves well made craft beers . . . or a close encounter with spirits of a different sort.

Sise Inn

An Elegant Bed and Breakfast Located on Court Street
With More Than a Few Ghostly Guests

The Sise Inn, located at 40 Court Street, is a beautifully restored Queen Anne-style home that has been converted into a charming bed-and-breakfast-style inn. The inn has thirty-four guest rooms, each decorated with Victorian-period antiques, or elegant reproductions that are indistinguishable from the real thing, and each room is complete with a style and atmosphere all its own. The house was originally built in 1881 for John Sise, a successful merchant, and it remained a private home until the 1930s. The house on Court Street has had a long and interesting history. It has been a private residence, a doctor's office, a beauty salon, and business offices. For a brief period of time, it was even used as a halfway house, which rumors have exaggerated into claiming it was a mental institution! The one label that has stuck to the building at Court Street through all its incarnations is that of local haunted house.

A small rocking chair located near the front desk has been known to rock excitedly back and forth, all on its own, and things often go missing from the front desk. In fact, things disappear and reappear so erratically from the front desk that most clerks make it a point to walk around holding items they need most often to do their job. They know that if they put it down and turn their back for even a minute, there is no guarantee the item will still be there when they turn back around. And once something is lost, it may appear in five minutes, five hours, or not at all.

The stairs leading up to the rooms from the lobby are as haunted as the front desk. They are well traveled by very audible ghostly footsteps. With all this ghostly activity you would think that the front desk clerks get used to bumps in the night pretty quickly, that there was nothing the haunted Sise Inn could throw at them that would faze them. This may be true to some degree, but at least one clerk was struck dumbfounded by one odd guest. On a proverbial dark and stormy night, a tall gruff man walked into the Inn, drenched in rain. Even before the man spoke, he gave off such an air of menace that the clerk decided to lie and tell him the Inn was full for the night.

"Is the lady Ghost here?" The man asked abruptly with a voice like broken glass grating, glaring at the front desk clerk.

The Sise Inn, a beautiful bed and breakfast that is as famous for its ghosts as it is for its inviting atmosphere.

The clerk hesitated. He had been expecting the man to ask for a room for the night and was taken aback by the sudden turn of conversation. For a moment he wondered if this was possibly a former resident of the Inn from back when it was a half-way house. Before he could make up his mind how to answer the strange question, the figure faded from sight. He had simply been another victim of the Sise Inn's many ghosts!

One hopes that whoever the menacing spirit was it is not the same ghost who gets a frisky with the Sise Inn maids. One former maid had a terrifying experience when she was hugged tightly by an invisible man with strong arms and pulled into a hallway closet. Another maid was folding bed sheets when she felt icy-cold hands grip her hips. She whirled around to confront the person but there was no one there. Other maids have reported feeling pinches and slaps from unseen hands as they went about their work cleaning up after guests.

Workers at the inn, male and female alike, also stay away from the elevators which tend to start and stop all on their own. One maid says she was trapped inside the rising and falling elevator for a good hour until she pleaded with the ghost to let her off, at which point the car stopped at the next floor and the doors opened easily. Handymen have never been able to find a mechanical reason for why the elevator sometimes acts this way.

Another time, guests who had been staying in the renovated carriage house, made it a point to approach the owner of the Inn to tell her how much they enjoyed seeing the maids dressed in period costumes as they went about their business. The surprised woman replied that she had never asked any employees to wear costumes to work, and that she certainly would have noticed if someone had taken up the practice! The guests protested that they had seen several women in Victorian garb walking around the grounds that day, but no other guests ever saw the figures and none of the maids would confess to such a trick.

Other Inn guests could have told the woman she'd gotten off lightly. One distraught guest showed up at the front desk in the middle of the night demanding he be given a new room in the nearly fully-booked Inn. When asked what the problem with his current room was, the guest explained that he'd looked up from the book he was reading just in time to see a potted plant hovering in mid-air. He watched the plant float there for several minutes when it suddenly flew around the perimeter of the room several times at high speed before being gently placed back in place. The beleaguered desk clerk didn't question the guest beyond that. Reservations were shifted around and the guest was given the keys to a new room on the other side of the building.

One night, when the Inn was empty of guests, the front desk clerk heard someone using the ice machine on the third floor. When the clerk went upstairs to investigate, he found a trail of water leading from the ice machine to guest room 204. When the door was opened by the curious clerk, a large pile of melting ice cubes were found sitting in the middle of the carpet.

This is not the only strange encounter to be reported in this room. Much of the ghostly activity at the Sise Inn centers around room 204. Many guests who have spent the night in that room wouldn't be surprised to hear the front desk clerk's story. More than a few of them have awoken in the middle of the night, hearing a heavy fist pounding on their room door, only to find a pile of ice cubes waiting for them when they open it. One woman was laying in the bed in 204 when the door opened by itself and the imprint of footsteps in the carpet were seen moving towards her. The woman then felt the invisible visitor lay on the bed with her. When she looked over there was the clear

Visitors to Room 204 sometimes get more than they bargained for at the Sise Inn.

shape of a man's body imprinted on the bedcovers—even though she could see she was alone in the room! Needless to say, the lady demanded other accommodations for the night.

Another of room 204's guests was inadvertently locked out of the room after they stepped out for a minute. Every time they placed their key in the door, it was pushed out roughly from the keyhole by something inside the locked room. The desk clerk was called up, but no one could get the key to work. A locksmith was finally summoned, and when he arrived, the door opened easily, no longer even locked. Inside, the room was filled with half-melted ice cubes— which the guest swore were not there when they'd stepped out earlier—but otherwise empty.

The key to room 204 is constantly misplaced, as though something wants the room to remain unoccupied. The Inn keeps many extra copies of the key on hand for just this reason. Oftentimes, after a guest loses their key to room 204, they arrive home and find it waiting for them at their own houses! It is a common occurrence for workers at the Sise Inn to get copies of the key for room 204 mailed to them by frightened guests.

Local legend gives two conflicting stories as to whom the lecherous ghost who likes to harass the maids is. Some say it is old John Sise himself who was supposed to have had an affair with one, or several, of his maids during his lifetime. There is an unverified rumor that he hung himself in what would later become room 204 when one of these maids fought off his advances and ran away with a butler with whom she was in love. Other stories say that it is the ghost of John Sise's butler. In these stories, the butler had a romantic relationship with one of the maids. When the maid broke things off with him, the butler killed her and then hung himself in the room. Like many of the hauntings in Portsmouth, it is hard to know where the truth lies in this story, and where local legends take over.

Psychics who have visited the Inn thave encountered several other specters. Many have felt or seen an arguing ghost couple who they trace back to a 1905 murder that took place several houses down from where the Sise Inn stands. A sailor returned home from a long sea voyage to find out that his wife had been unfaithful with the caretaker the sailor had hired to watch over the house for him while he was away. In a pique of anger, the man killed both his wife and her lover before killing himself. The killer and his adulterous wife's spirits both haunted the house where the crime took place until it was demolished many years later. Some psychics have theorized that, at this time, the unhappy couple moved to 40 Court Street because they were comforted by how much it looked like the time period they had lived in. Proponents of this theory point out that the missing room keys could be the work of the spirit of the murdered wife, forever trying to keep her angry husband locked out of the room she takes refuge in.

Despite the tales of love gone sour, adultery, suicide, and murder, the Sise Inn is a first-class place to stay. Many people who are guests of the Inn will walk away from their stay with nothing more to say about it other than how great the service was. Of those who do end up with an unusual encounter, only very few people will actually feel frightened of the ghosts at the Sise Inn. The amorous ghost is seen as more of a jokester than anything else and the missing room keys and antics with the ice machine are more annoying than terrifying.

Voices From Beyond the Grave

ne of the most common, strangest, and some say possibly the most dangerous supernatural phenomena people experience is "Electronic Voice Phenomena" (more commonly called EVP). This phenomenon is also known under a slew of other names, among them such acronyms as "Electronic Disturbance Phenomena" (EDP) and the more New Age sounding moniker of "Trans-Dimensional Communication" (TDC).

EVPs, no matter what they are called, are voices and sounds that are captured by recording equipment even though they, usually, are inaudible at the time of recording. This includes voices that appear on tape recordings of unoccupied rooms and voices that seem to manifest out of the so-called white noise sounds of electrical appliances such as TV static or fan hums. Instrumental TransCommunication (ITC) is a broader umbrella term that EVPs fall under. ITCs are any communications from the spirit world that use any kind of electronic piece of technology. This term applies to both auditory and visual forms of communication—the erratic static of a television set that briefly seems to form cohesive images, for example, or strange outputs from a computer printer or fax machine. The scientific community discounts ITCs in the same way they try to debunk EVPs.

Looking at it historically, EVPs appeared pretty much as soon as there was recording equipment available to capture them. People have always been interested in "proving" there is life after death and modern technologies such as cameras and recorders were quickly applied to these efforts. Many people who are interested in the supernatural feel that the use of modern technologies adds a respectable air of science to their goal of demonstrating that ghosts are real phenomena. However, the scientific community has always been quick to distance themselves from any of these attempts. Even those who believe in the extraordinary nature of EVPs don't always agree that they are caused by ghosts. People have proposed that EVPs are caused by everything from alien transmissions to the thoughts of perfectly normal human beings who are asleep. Some of these more outlandish theories that have been linked to EVPs only work to make the scientific community want to distance themselves even more from the phenomena.

The earliest well publicized EVPs were made by the American photographer Attila von Szalay who, in the 1950s, experimented with several different ways of tuning into the frequencies of the dead. Von Szalay tried everything from record players to custom-made equipment involving sound-proofed cabinets that managed to record such "otherworldly" message as "Hot Dog, Art!" and "Merry Christmas to you all!" As silly as these spirit messages seem, Von Szalay wrote several articles that would go on to be published by a variety of at least half-way respectable journals. His journalistic success garnered him a book contract which resulted in him co-authoring a book on the subject of EVPs.

Believe it or not. Von Szalay's messages are a little easier to swallow as true accounts of communing with the dead then some of the other more famous recordings and recording devices. In the early 1980s, William O'Neil, a stockbroker of some note, held a press conference where he announced he had created an audio device that allowed the living to converse quite easily with the dead. O'Neil took no credit for the invention, attributing its design to a scientist who had died half a dozen years earlier. O'Neil, it was announced, had been transmitted the design psychically. At this press conference, O'Neil offered up instructions on how to build a "Spiricom," free of charge, to any researchers who were interested in verifying his claims. Unfortunately, no other researcher was able to get the results from their Spiricoms that O'Neil claimed to get from his. He was dismissed generally as a fraud, or possibly mentally unstable, but a few stalwart supporters felt that O'Neil's success with the device was linked to some sort of high level of psychic ability that he possessed that was lacking in every other Spiricom builder.

With all of these unusual claims, it is no surprise that EVPs are largely ignored by the scientific community. Skeptics often pass off EVPs as recordings of stray radio or television signals, possibly even recordings of cell phone conversations. We've all heard the urban legend about the man who thought he was going crazy because he kept hearing voices only to discover that his dental work was picking up a late-night radio talk show. EVPs can easily be seen as the paranormal equivalent of that old tale. So it is easy to dismiss EVPs as something similar.

However, anyone who actually captures one of these recordings or listens to one, will be hard pressed to explain them away so easily. The voices are, most often, indistinct and hard to understand on top of that because each syllable sounds as though it is being said at vastly different speeds. Many times, the voices recorded will respond to the words being spoken by the living people in the room—even if those people heard no voices at the time of the recording! But most often EVPs are normally very brief, a single word or short phrase, and have no connection to anything going on in the real world.

Even if experts don't always see eye to eye when talking about what EVPS really are, the one thing they can all agree on is that people need to be very careful with EVPs. They are not to be depended on. Those who see no ghostly side to them worry that they are messages from the listeners own subconscious, possibly saying things they are not ready to hear and confront. Even if you accept that EVPs are messages from spirits, you have no real way of knowing if the voice you've recorded is of a loved one trying to pass you a message from the other side, or a spectral jokester who may have an agenda of his own. In many cases, it seems the voices are not even trying to directly communicate with the living and that the recording has simply picked up on a conversation between a group of spirits that has little or nothing to do with the world of the living.

The 2005 movie White Noise, the plot centering around EVPs, chillingly ends with the warning that every one in twelve EVP recordings are threatening in nature. However, it is unclear exactly where the filmmakers got this "fact" and many experts in the field of parapsychology have publicly disputed these numbers. Interestingly, the most common EVP captured is the sound of a barking dog. Some people have not only captured the pet, but also what seems to be the voice of its master issuing commands to sit, to speak, and sometimes to please stop all that barking!

Tape recorders are one of the basic tools of the ghost hunter, hobbyist, and professional alike. If you are interested in capturing some EVPs of your own, they are easy enough to try and do. All you need is any kind of recording device—the debate rages on if digital recorders are better or worse—and patience. Then, all you have to do is leave your recorder in an empty room. Most experts will tell you to then leave the room for the length of the tape in the recorder. By doing this you can ensure that any odd noises your recorder picks up won't be from you moving around the room.

Once you have more experience with ghost hunting or if you have a sensitivity for ghosts, you can attempt a question and answer type of recording. To do this, after setting up your recorder, wait until you sense that spirits may be nearby. Once you get that feeling, politely invite the spirits to join you. Then begin to ask a list of questions in a loud clear voice. It is likely that you will hear nothing after asking your questions. If so, don't get discouraged. Just keep on asking questions, pausing in-between so your ghost has time to reply. You may find when you play the tape back afterwards that you can distinctly hear voices replying to your questions, even if you heard nothing at the time you made the recording.

It is always important to be polite and gracious when trying to communicate with the dead. Proper manners will get you much further than belligerence or threats.

Quite often when playing back the recording, you may hear a noise but not one that sounds anything like someone speaking. If this occurs, try playing the tape back at different speeds. Once you've slowed down, or sped up the tape, the voices may become clearer to you. You might even have to play the tape backwards in order to hear the voices properly. Do not be surprised if out of many questions, only one or two get answered, or if the answers seem to have little relation to the questions you asked. Sometimes, the meanings of the answers you get will become clear as time goes on or once you begin to research the history of the place where you made your tape.

A Last Goodbye

Amanda's four sisters liked to call her the caboose. She was the youngest of the five children in her family, separated from the next oldest by close to eight years. This not only meant that she got the luxury of feeling like an only child, since her sisters were so much older and during her lifetime, one by one, they all moved away from home, but also that her parents were already quite old by the time she made her unexpected appearance.

By the time she was ready for college, all of her sisters were married and had moved away. It was about this time that her mother's health began to fail. Amanda made the tough decision to attend a smaller local college so she could keep on living at home and help take care of her parents. Her sisters tried to help as much as possible, but they all had their own families and lives, and besides, Amanda seemed naturally inclined to the role of caretaker.

Her father was active enough to maintain the small yard and the outside of their small middle-class house in one of Portsmouth's residential neighborhoods. Amanda took over the housekeeping inside the home. She didn't mind the work, but it always drove her crazy how stuck in their ways her parents were. Everything in their house was so 1980s! They didn't have a DVD player and they still used an old-style answering machine rather then just pay a little more for voicemail with their phone service. It hadn't bugged her so much before, when she thought she'd be leaving for college in a few years, but now that it looked like she would be spending at least her college years still living at home, she wanted to upgrade things a bit.

Amanda's father was not in as much of a hurry to start changing things as she was. They even fought about it a few times. But all the fighting and talk of changes stopped when Amanda's mother became so ill she had to go to the hospital. There was just enough time for all of Amanda's sisters, their husbands, and the assorted grandchildren to come and say goodbye to her before she passed away forever.

The funeral was stressful and exhausting. Amanda's father had gone to the hotel where her sisters' families were all staying to say goodbye to his grandchildren. As Amanda walked through the front door, she saw the answering machine light frantically blinking red. It had gotten over a dozen messages during the few hours they were at the funeral home. Amanda really didn't want to listen to more platitudes and condolences from friends and family but she figured if she didn't listen to them now she would never work up the energy and then her Dad would be left with the task.

Pushing the play button Amanda was surprised to hear an immediate beep as the first message appeared to be a hang up and the machine turned over to the next message. BEEP.

Beep. . .Beep. . .Beep. . .

It went on and on, through each message. Every one that came up would play for only a few seconds, no sounds could be heard at all from the caller, before being cut off and moving to the next one. Who would call a dozen times and just keep on hanging up on the day of her Mothers funeral? Maybe the out-of-date machine was broken?

Amanda was just about to hit the delete button and erase the faulty tape when, at the very last second, she thought she heard something that made her pause. Instead of hitting delete she hit the rewind button and turned the volume on the machine way up.

Beep. . . Beep. . . Beep. . .

After many hang ups the tape wound its way to the spot where she had thought she'd heard something. As the noise started again Amanda turned the volume up even more.

"Mandie?" The voice on the tape began, jerkily, and near a whisper. "Thank you."

The voice was sketchy and jerky. But it was, unmistakably, her mother's voice.

Amanda kept rewinding the tape and playing it back, over and over again, waiting for something in her brain to click and for her to decide it was one of her sister's voices or that the tape was blank after all. But each time she played it, she became more and more certain that it was her mother's voice.

As she heard her father come up the porch stairs, one of her sisters in tow talking gently to him, Amanda popped the tape out of the answering machine and ran upstairs to her room with it. She didn't want anyone to accidentally erase the message or for her father to hear it. She was just so glad she had never convinced him to switch over to voice mail.

The Imaginary Friend

Beth and John weren't surprised at all when they moved into their new home and their four-year-old daughter started talking to someone they couldn't see. Imaginary friends are a normal part of most childhoods and, after all, they had just moved. If the imaginary friend gave their daughter, Mindy, a feeling of security and eased the transition from apartment to house, that was fine by them.

But as time went on, they were surprised by the depth of Mindy's imaginary play. The unseen friend could easily make the little girl erupt into giggles and even startle her on a few occasions. Beth was very surprised one day when she watched Mindy and her imaginary friend, "Joseph," play hide and go seek for several hours. Could it really be that much fun to pretend someone was hiding from you or finding you that you would do it for so long, Beth wondered.

When it was time for Mindy to begin kindergarten, the little girl asked if Joseph would be going to school with her. Beth suddenly had a dilemma. She did want to make the jump to school easy on her little girl but she also didn't want the other kids to think her little girl was weird. Would Mindy be so caught up in playing with "Joseph" that she wouldn't even try to make friends with the real kids at school? Finally, she told Mindy that Joseph would have to stay home while she was at school during the day. Beth was surprised at how well her little girl took the news.

Maybe, thought Beth, she's outgrowing Joseph. Maybe, when she has more kids her own age to play with she won't need this imaginary friend anymore.

Mindy's first day of school went off without a hitch. The little girl was excited to go and Beth managed to help her onto the school bus without any tears. Mindy came home excited about her school day and all the kids she had met. Even so, the first thing she did when she came home from school, after greeting her mother, was to go find Joseph. Beth heard her telling him all about her school day and the kids there. Beth was surprised Mindy still kept up the illusion of Joseph, but still saw no real harm in it. When Mindy was ready, she knew the little girl would give up her imaginary friend.

A few weeks into the school year things started to get strange inside the house when Mindy wasn't there. Sometimes Beth was sure she wasn't alone in a room, even though she could plainly see no one else was there. For the first time since they had moved to Portsmouth, she started locking the doors when she was alone in the house during the day, even though it didn't help calm her nerves any. She got so paranoid that she had trouble sleeping at nights and instead began napping during the day while Mindy was at school.

Beth found herself awoken from one of these cat naps when the TV clicked on by itself. The bright burst of static woke her up instantly. But just as soon as she was awake, she decided she must still be asleep and dreaming. In the white noise of the old television she could swear she was seeing a face!

Faintly, in the constantly moving white and black static, she saw what was unmistakably that of a young boy, a boy just about her daughter's age as best she could tell. As she stared at the image horrified, she saw its lips were moving slowly as though the boy was carefully enunciating each word for her benefit so she could read his lips without struggle. The longer she stared, the more sure she was that the boy was mouthing, "It's too quiet with Mindy gone."

In a rush, Beth leapt off the couch and turned the TV off. When she would turn it on again, she was always careful to make sure she put it on an actual station and not let it linger too long on the dead channels in-between. Beth was never able to totally convince herself that what she saw was real, but she started the habit of playing Mindy's Disney CDs when the girl was at school and all the ghostly activity in the house calmed down immediately.

The Apple Tree

The apple tree in Jeff's backyard was something of an oddity. It was the only apple tree in the neighborhood and its gnarled twisted branches inspired ghost stories from the kids who lived in the houses on either side of Jeff's Portsmouth home. He always had the idea that the branches were supposed to be trimmed to encourage fruiting but he wasn't sure the correct way to do this so, year after year, he let the tree grow more and more convoluted. Of course, those who knew Jeff well knew his lack of expertise was only a convenient excuse. The truth was that the tree freaked Jeff out a little bit. Or maybe more than a little bit.

The area around the apple tree always seemed a little bit cooler than the air around it and sometimes people complained of feeling a near tangible cold spot roaming around the tree's trunk. Eerily, when Jeff was out back doing yard work, whenever he went near the tree, his lawn mower or weed whacker would sputter and die out.

But the strangest incident occurred when Jeff was having a barbeque at his house one Fourth of July. He broke out his video camera to tape the event. He moved around the yard trying to capture everything and everyone. It didn't occur to him to avoid the apple tree until he was already standing beneath it. But luck was with him. The camera didn't short out the way his yard tools always seemed to.

Things may have seemed normal enough while he was taping but it was a different story when he played the tape back. The tape reliably played back the sunny afternoon party up until the moment that Jeff mistakenly stepped beneath the apple tree. The instant that he moved into its shadow, the playback went strange. The colors seemed to bleed and intensify, a lurid unrealistic Technicolor bleed not found in nature . . . or anywhere else on the tape! Then static started up, the images breaking up and stuttering. Worst of all, the sound became a squeal—it hurt to listen to it. But somewhere in the cacophony, Jeff could make out voices.

> " . . . down the avenue. . ."
> "You are alone."
> "I'm ready . . . ."

Then, on screen, Jeff moved away from the apple tree and instantly the tape snapped back to normal. Confused, he sat through the rest of the video but it played out fine with no disturbances whatsoever. Jeff replayed the thing a couple of times, slowing things down every time he came to the strange part of the video. His first instinct was simply that the phrases he heard—the phrases he didn't remember hearing anyone speak—were just things that he had missed people saying. But the voices definitely didn't sound like any of his friends or family and all he had to do was watch the tape to see that no one had been standing anywhere near him when he caught that piece of tape. Everyone at the party seemed, subconsciously at least, to have felt the same way he did about the apple tree and to have avoided it as well.

Jeff had owned the recorder for a long time and had never had a problem with it. He racked his brain trying to figure out what could have happened. He even brought it in to be serviced, but no one found anything wrong with it. The odd tape piqued his interest enough so that he started to experiment, bringing a regular audio recorder under the tree at different times of the day and varying weather conditions to see what he would pick up.

In time, Jeff would come to find three different distinct voices that the tapes picked up pretty regularly, although every so often he would capture the voices of strangers. The three regulars, as he came to think of them, never seemed to be speaking to each other and he never felt like they were trying to tell him anything either. Eventually, he grew bored with the whole thing. He ended up with reams of tape full of voices saying the most mundane things imaginable.

Jeff never really managed to convince himself that what he was picking up was the voices of the dead but his unusual hobby certainly sparked a lot of conversations and debates when he had barbeques in the backyard.

The Glass-Breaking Ghost

Familiar Family Ghost Talks About New Neighbor

Sherry knew from the first time she ever stepped foot in her house that it was haunted. But unlike a lot of people, Sherry felt that the home's ghost was a selling point, not a detraction. Sherry was no novice when it came to living in a haunted house. By the time she bought the split-level ranch in Portsmouth, she had already lived in six different haunted homes and apartments, including the old farmhouse she had grown up in. That house had boasted no less than four different spirits and Sherry had never seen any reason to be scared of a one of them. She always liked to say that you weren't living in a true New England house if it didn't have a spook or two.

The ghost at Sherry's house seemed to be that of an old woman. It was obvious that the woman must have been a former owner of the home and that she had loved it very much. Because the spirit most often manifested itself in the living room, which was bedecked with soft floral wallpaper, Sherry's children dubbed the spirit "Aunt Rose." Aunt Rose was a protective spirit who started off watching over the house and, in time, started to look after the family as though they were her own. When the lights went out during a storm, Aunt Rose was credited with putting the emergency candles and flashlights out on the kitchen table for the family to find easily in the dark. When the kids got a little older and tried to sneak TV shows they knew they weren't supposed to watch, Aunt Rose had the habit of turning the television set off at the juiciest parts. When the last of the children had grown up and left for college, Sherry swore she felt Aunt Rose's gentles arms wrap around her shoulder in a comforting squeeze.

Many years after Sherry moved into her home, the house next door went up for sale. Sherry didn't like to think ill of anyone, but she was happy to see the old neighbors go. Early on, when she had first moved in, a quiet feud had started between her household and these neighbors when they had chopped down a lovely willow tree at the edge of Sherry's property to put their fence in. Sherry had loved the tree and it had clearly been on her side of the property divide. If they had asked, she probably could have been persuaded to chop the tree down so they could fence in their in ground pool, but since they had done it without asking, deep down she couldn't seem to forgive them. She was excited when she saw the house sell and a moving van pull in a few weeks later. She was determined to get off on the right foot with this new addition to the neighborhood.

Sherry gave the new neighbor a few days to settle in and then invited him over for brunch. The brunch went well; she was happy to see she had quite a bit in common with the neighbor. But Sherry was a little embarrassed when the glass of iced tea she handed him cracked down the side as soon as he grasped it. The man apologized profusely, but Sherry could certainly see that it wasn't anything that he had done. She was just glad he hadn't sliced his finger when the glass broke, or gotten his pants wet when the iced tea began to dribble out!

The man ended up being a great person to live next door to. He was quiet and friendly and kept both his house and his lawn well maintained. But every time Sherry had him over to her place, her glasses cracked when he picked them up. It ended up being something of a joke between them. He would share some lemonade out on the porch but never inside the house. Any time they did, she ended up with ruined glassware and he was never able to slake his thirst.

The occurrence was so absurd, the only explanation Sherry could come up with for it was that it was something that was Aunt Rose's doing. But Aunt Rose, or any of the ghosts that Sherry had experience with, had never broken anything before. What did it mean?

Sherry's worst fear was that it was Aunt Rose's way of warning her about her new neighbor. But why? He was such a nice man and such a better neighbor than the last ones to occupy that house. Sherry tried asking Aunt Rose what the problem with the neighbor was, hoping the spirit would leave her some clue, but if Aunt Rose ever replied to the questions, Sherry couldn't tell.

Worried that her neighbor was harboring a secret side of himself that Aunt Rose was trying to warn her about, Sherry decided she had to find out why the glasses kept breaking when he came by. She asked around town and eventually was directed to a psychic who was supposed to know about these sorts of things. Sherry didn't like the idea of a psychic in her house; she secretly feared the woman would scare Aunt Rose away and Sherry was of no mind to get rid of the spirit that had been so faithful to her family for so many years, but she did ask the woman if she had ever heard of anything like this before.

The psychic hadn't but she had a few good theories as to why Aunt Rose was cracking those glasses. She said that most hauntings of this type, ones that started up suddenly or changed so drastically after so many years and centering around a specific person, could be because the person reminded the spirit of someone who had been important to them in life. If this was the case, than Aunt Rose probably didn't mean to keep on breaking the glasses and probably felt sorry when she did. But, like an over-excited child, she was breaking them accidentally because she was so worked up over seeing someone she thought she recognized. Since Sherry was convinced that Aunt Rose had been a mother when she was alive, perhaps she was mistaking the next door neighbor for her son or grandchild.

The other explanation the psychic offered was that the next door neighbor may have been psychic himself and didn't even realize it. Aunt Rose would get very upset if she "met" someone who she felt should sense her that didn't acknowledge her, the same as any living person would get vexed if they walked into a room and one person made it a point to ignore them. Aunt Rose may have been breaking the glasses out of frustration that the neighbor wouldn't pay attention to her or she might have been cracking them in order to catch his attention.

Whatever the reason, glasses kept on breaking as long as the neighbor tried to drink from them. Sherry soon purchased a plastic cup for him to use when he came over to her house and the broken glassware continued to be something of an inside joke for them. If he had been hiding a darker side, Sherry never saw it. The man was a great neighbor until he passed away himself a few years later.

New Hampshire Community Technical College at Pease International Tradeport

Former Hospital Home to Odd Occurrences on Abandoned Top Floors

New Hampshire Community Technical College at Pease International Tradeport. NHCTC: education, lunch, ghosts.

New Hampshire Community Technical College is located at Pease International Tradeport, which until it was closed due to budget cutbacks in the early 1990s, was Pease Air Force Base. This 4,365-acre plot of land continues to be the home of the New Hampshire Air National Guard but, today, is mainly known as an industrial and business complex. It is home to something in the nature of 150 different businesses and, of course, the New Hampshire Community Technical College.

The College is housed in a former air force hospital. The top two floors of this building have been left unoccupied. They are not suitable for classrooms and the elevator that stops to them have been disabled so students can't wander up there by accident. But from outside the building, you'd never know those floors are inaccessible to people. Lights on these floors shut on and off by themselves regularly and the dark shapes of people can be seen passing by the windows, and sometimes even stopping to peer outside.

One student, who was at the building late one evening, reports that one of these phantom figures, who appeared to be an astonishing seven feet tall, not only stooped to stare through the window, but it also raised one massive hand to wave a greeting to her. Having heard the tales of the ghosts that plague this building, she left quickly and decided not to try and investigate. She is now careful to never be alone even on the floors that house classrooms and she never lingers in the parking lot when evening begins to fall. She even goes so far as to always park in the front of the building, which is devoid of the windows that line the sides, just to make sure she never sees anything frightening again.

From the floor immediately below these abandoned levels, the sound of many footsteps are heard endlessly walking back and forth, back and forth. Some maintenance workers who have been sent

Seen from the outside it is easy to tell that this building was formerly used as a hospital.

upstairs to check out the noises say they've felt an overwhelming sense that they should get out or leave as soon as they'd unlocked the doors leading to those areas.

One long-time maintenance worker says the ghostly activity used to be much more, well, active many years before. It has quieted down since the building went through its last major renovation project. This worker used to be surprised by the figure of a little old man quite often. The elderly ghost paid no attention to the living he came across, but paced the upper floors of the building ceaselessly. He is described as being rotund, short on stature, with wild white hair, and a grandfatherly grin. So far, at least, there have been no public theories passed around as to whom this spirit may have been in life.

The Sheafe Street Inn

Ghostly Horses and Troubled Artists at One of Portsmouth's Oldest Inns, and the Spirit Chef at Ceres Bakery.

The Inn

Until recent times, the Sheafe Street Inn had always been used as an inn and tavern. Today, the inn is apartments and the tavern has been converted into a bakery. But it is so filled with haunts, it's a wonder there is any room left for tenants or bakers!

This sign still hangs outside the building, located at the corner of Sheafe Street and Penhallow Street, though the Sheafe Street Inn is currently used as an apartment building.

One of the most famous former residents of The Sheafe Street Inn is thought to be one of the many ghosts that plague the building. Kittery, Maine, native John Haley Bellamy was, and is, one of the premier wood cavers in the United States. He is most known for his wall-hanging eagle carvings. John Bellamy himself did not consider what he did true art and never signed his pieces. But Bellamy eagles, as his pieces have come to be known, are so distinctive that collectors have little trouble identifying his work. One of his best known works is the "Lancaster Eagle Figurehead," a 3,200-pound carved eagle with an eighteen-foot wingspan that now resides in the Mariners Museum in Newport News, Virginia. In an auction recently, a Bellamy eagle went for more than a half a million dollars, and it is common for his works(of any size) to go for at least one hundred thousand. This is pretty ironic considering that in his lifetime Bellamy often worked for as little as $2.50 a day.

Despite his talent and the relative fame he achieved in his lifetime, Bellamy was a deeply troubled man. Though much of his life was spent in Kittery, he traveled restlessly throughout New Hampshire and Massachusetts seeking work. He had relatives who owned the Sheafe Street Inn and often stayed with them when he was working at the Portsmouth Naval Yard. On April 16, 1914, John Haley Bellamy died while staying with these relatives, and ever since his death, his ghost has been reported in the room where he passed away.

Bottles of liquor that are left in this room are quickly smashed, along with drinking glasses, although there is little evidence that John Bellamy was a teetotaler in life. His spirit also roams constantly around the room opening and shutting windows. John Bellamy seems to be as restless in death as he was in life, but tied to this nineteenth-century house for reasons we cannot fathom.

He seems to have plenty of ghostly company though, for his is not the only active spirit roaming this building. A former owner of the Inn, who kept a bedroom for herself on the first floor, was startled one night when she was shoved out of bed by icy hands. Terrified, she fled for safety in a neighbor's home. When the neighbor went to investigate, he found the Inn locked up tight and perfectly empty. Other people spending the night in this same room have experienced similar rough treatment. Today, the space is no longer used as bedroom and instead is a comfortable breakfast nook in a spacious apartment. The ghost only seems to enjoy disturbing sleepers, though. There have been no reports of it smashing dishes in the breakfast nook. Since the room has been converted to an apartment, this spirit has faded into the background.

Over the years, sailors in particular have been mishandled by the ghosts at the Sheafe Street Inn for some reason. Many, on leave for the weekend and out enjoying everything that Portsmouth had to offer, found themselves tossed to the ground by an unseen force as they walked by the building. A few felt the force so distinctively, and so heavily, that they swore someone must have jumped out of a second floor window on top of them. Only after being shown the locked and unoccupied rooms could they be convinced they had been attacked by something from out of this world. Inside the tavern, it was not unusual for fights to break out because the sailors could never be convinced it was a ghost who had jumped them and not a drunken townie.

One evening, as a guest was leaving the Inn, he heard a low whistle and the barking of many dogs. When he turned to find the source of the noise, he saw a ghost dressed in equestrian gear, waving a cutlass, and surrounded by a wild rowdy pack of twenty hunting dogs. Later on, a group of five people reported seeing the same horseman and his dogs walk out of a bank of fog. This unusual specter was the cause of much speculation and if it hadn't been seen more than once, it might have been passed off as imagination. But many years later, during a remodeling of the Sheafe Street Inn, equestrian gear matching that seen worn by the spirit was found hidden in one of the original walls

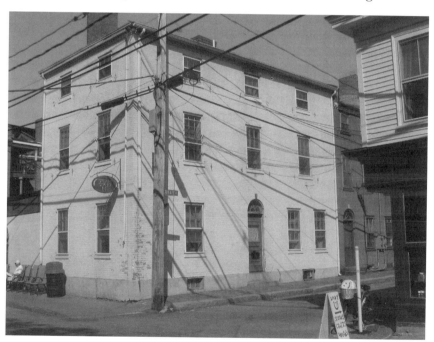

The ghosts at The Sheafe Street Inn aren't just confined to the building itself. People walking by on the street below have been accosted by both a violent spirit who seems to attack from the second floor windows, and a ghostly rider and pack of dogs hunting something inexplicable through the streets of Portsmouth.

of the building. No one can find an explanation for who this ghost may have been in life or why these items were hidden in the wall. It is a true mystery, that will probably never be solved—that is, unless this ghost decides to suddenly start to speak!

The Bakery

What was once the Sheafe Street Inn's tavern is now Ceres Bakery, a Portsmouth landmark that moved to this location back in 1983. They probably didn't realize that the kitchen came complete with prank-pulling specters. Many of the Ceres employees have complained of feeling a presence in the bakery with them, especially when there after hours. Oftentimes, the crew comes in to find the kitchen in disarray in the morning, even when they themselves picked up and cleaned the night before. Some have even had things disappear off the counters just in the small space of time it takes for them to walk from one side of the kitchen to another and back again. Workers sometimes come in to find every drawer in the kitchen pulled out and emptied onto the floor or for all of the hanging pots and pans to be tossed around the counters after closing.

The activity seemed to peak in the mid 1990s during a time of expansion and renovation in the attached Sheafe Street Inn. Things calmed down some after the construction was done, but cooks at the bakery still sometimes catch glimpses of movement from the corners of their eyes when they are at work in the kitchen.

The tavern attached to The Sheafe Street Inn has long been plagued by prank playing phantoms. It has been a bakery since the 1980s, but that doesn't seem to have made a difference to the ghosts.

The Old North Cemetery

In 1798, Thomas Sheafe's ship, the Mentor, sailed into Portsmouth Harbor. It came laden with sugar, coffee, tobacco, molasses, and disease. The boat had come into port from the Caribbean island, Martinique, unknowingly bringing with it the dreaded yellow fever.

Yellow fever has been the source of many devastating epidemics throughout history. In modern day, there is a yellow fever vaccine available, but the disease is still a problem is many African countries where prices are high and demand outranks supplies. The World Heath Organization estimates that currently yellow fever kills 30,000 people each year, and infects hundreds of thousands of others. In modern days, we know that the disease is spread, usually, through a mosquito bite. However, historically, little was known about how the disease was caused or spread.

In the eighteenth century, the disease-carrying mosquitoes were plentiful in the Caribbean and, when they were accidentally transported to the northeast United States on ships like Mentor, they found a plethora of wetlands and swamps to breed in. There were quarantine laws in Portsmouth during the eighteenth century, however, they were generally disregarded by incoming ships since they were not usually enforced by the city. Financially, too much depended on ships carrying perishable goods as quickly as possible from port to port and even where quarantine laws were followed, bribes and connections could help pass any ship through the process with little more than a second look.

Symptoms of yellow fever do not appear for up to a week after infection and the early symptoms are generally mundane and easy to confuse with almost any lesser-common ailments. People infected complain of backaches, muscle aches, loss of appetite and nausea—all things that most people would complain of after spending months or years at sea. It is usually not until a week or so later that more serious symptoms surface and the patient starts to take on the jaundiced look that gives the disease its colorful name.

So, it is not surprising that when the sailors aboard the Mentor started getting sick, no one noticed much. Being aboard a ship for months at a time leaves people open to a host of nutritional and viral ailments. It was not until the merchant Thomas Sheafe's own children, who had not been aboard the ship, fell ill that anyone realized the disease might be something more serious. And by that point, it was too late to stop the spread of the illness. It would not be until three months later, when the first frost came and killed off the mosquito population, that the spread of the yellow fever was halted.

About ten percent of the population in Portsmouth died as a result of this yellow fever epidemic. These bodies were all buried in a mass grave in what we now call Old North Cemetery, a burying ground that also features the final resting pots of several prominent Portsmouth historical figures.

Old North has something of a reputation for being not very well maintained. Visitors to the historic cemetery usually comment on the trash seen littering the gravestones and pathways. There has been a strong movement lately to clean up the burial grounds and make it a more prominent tourist stop.

The local ghost tours do sometimes bring tourists on by to view the grounds at Old North. They are drawn by the strange unearthly wailing sometimes heard echoing throughout the cemetery. It is thought to be the distressed cries of the yellow plague victims who are upset at their hasty and unmarked internment.

Be Careful What You Wish For

A Ghost-Hunting Hobbyist Gets the Encounter of a Lifetime

Ghost hunting had always been a hobby for Christine, just something to do on the weekends with a few friends who also loved the paranormal. It started off innocently enough. Each October, when the haunted walking tours started up in Portsmouth, she and her friends went on all of them. After exhausting the paranormal tourist experiences that Portsmouth had to offer, they eventually decided to start their own informal ghost-hunting group.

They began by poking around some of Portsmouth's more famous haunts, the ones the walking tours had already pointed out to them, equipped with disposable cameras and tape recorders. Then they moved on to the homes of friends who swore they thought their houses were haunted. In time, word got around about the group and they started getting phone calls from home owners and landlords asking them to investigate their own odd happenings. The group had a bad experience on one of these trips; it ended with an irate homeowner upset at them for not being able to "fix" his ghostly troubles, and unable to understand that the group didn't promise to fix anything, but simply to record and document what was happening and offer their advice. It wasn't a big deal, but the experience seemed to sour things with the group and they soon stopped their get-togethers.

Everyone else seemed really disappointed when the group stopped meeting, but secretly Christine was relieved. She just loved reading scary stories and watching shows like Ghosthunters on the Sci-Fi Channel. But Christine didn't know if she really believed in ghosts. Everyone else in the group seemed so sure that ghosts were real and that they were somehow going to get proof of it. They never even stopped to discuss if the stories they were hearing were true or if ghosts could, possibly, not exist outside of TV shows and books. Christine liked to think they were true stories, but deep in her heart she was a skeptic.

Secretly, she had hoped that her ghost-hunting group would find something to finally and truly prove to her that ghosts did exist. But it never seemed to happen for them. Oh, sure, they had gotten plenty to orb photographs, small fuzzy-colored splotches that appeared on film even when they hadn't been visible at the time in real life, and she had even thought she'd brushed up against the dense cold spots of air that many people thought were the physical manifestations of ghosts that couldn't be seen with the naked eye. Sometimes though Christine worried that she was only trying to convince herself that this was proof and that really there was perfectly good explanations for the occurrences—explanations that had nothing to do with the spirits of the dearly departed. Everyone else in her group just seemed so positive about everything they saw, or thought they saw, and she was a little afraid to bring up her doubts to anyone else.

Sometimes, even after the group broke up, Christine would occasionally still get phone calls from people asking to have their homes investigated. Christine turned them all down politely but firmly. Within a few weeks, the calls mostly stopped. So she was surprised several months later when, out of the blue, she got another phone call from a frantic homeowner asking her to come and take a look at his basement. Christine hesitated between ignoring the call and calling him back and going through the whole "the group broke up" story again. She didn't want to be rude, but she really just wanted to put the whole thing behind her.

The next day she received another call from the same guy.

The third day, before she even had a chance to respond to that message, he left two more. Each one was more frantic than the last. On the fourth message he left, along with his name, two contact numbers, an email address, and his home address. Something about the home address seemed to flip a switch on in Christine's mind, but she couldn't think why.

After much pondering, and a trip to her filing cabinet to look through her old day book, Christine realized that the address sounded familiar because, before going belly up, her ghost-hunting group had received two phone calls about investigating the same address, each one from a different owner. And both those owners seemed to have no link to the new owner calling her repeatedly right now. The house had acquired three different owners in under a year?

Suddenly Christine was interested.

She found herself in her backroom digging out all her old ghost-hunting equipment, the video recorders, tape recorders, and cameras. She thought about calling some of the members of her old group to come along but didn't want to start the whole group going again. She figured if they went out to one house, they'd keep on going out to more. Christine called back the homeowner and set up a time to come by and check out the house, but she didn't call any of her old ghost-hunting friends.

Driving up to the house, Christine couldn't help but feel that she was wasting her time. It was located on a sunny residential road filled with modern, non-descript homes. The directions the home owner had given her brought her to the front door an unassuming two-story home, with a glassed-in front porch, which looked almost exactly like every other house on the street. Across the road, two young kids played Frisbee with their dog, while an older woman next door stared at them grumpily watering her flowers. There were other kids riding bikes, a pair of young mothers pushing strollers, and in the background, Christine could hear the purring hum of a lawnmower. It was middle class wholesome as any place could be and, it seemed, the most unlikely place in the world to be haunted. Sure, she knew hauntings happened in regular houses all the time, probably more often than they happened in scary cemeteries or abandoned farmhouses. But this place was just so . . . normal.

Inside the house, Christine barely heard a thing the homeowner, indeed the third in less then a year, had to say. When she did tune in, it was the typical non-sense cold spots, keys disappearing then reappearing, footsteps in the basement when he knew no one else was home. It was all as typical as the sunny day outside. Christine looked around the green wallpapered kitchen, brightly lit with its eastward-facing windows and a row of fluorescent light bulbs, and thought she had never been any place that had felt less haunted in her entire life. After a few minutes, she realized that the homeowner had stopped talking and was looking at her funny.

"Um, I guess I'll start in the basement and work my way upstairs," Christine said lamely, trying to cover up the fact that she hadn't been listening.

The homeowner led her down the rickety wooden steps into the basement. It was stifling hot down there, with nothing but one bare light bulb and two dirty half windows to let in the light. Slowly, thinking how futile it all was, Christine started to unpack her tape recorder and camera. Upstairs, a phone began to ring and the homeowner excused himself to go and answer it.

Once he was gone, Christine stopped even pretending to go through the motions and sat down on a dusty stool. She looked glumly around the gloomy basement. There were old chairs missing their backs, piled in one corner. A few tools and a half unwound ball of string on the table behind her. She could see soft yellow light pouring down the stairs towards her. Suddenly, a dark shape passed in front of this light coming from the kitchen.

"I guess I'm done down here," said Christine, holding her tape recorder and camera in her hands.

When she got no reply she started walking up the wooden stairs, thinking the homeowner didn't hear her. She was startled to find a young girl at the top of the stairs, staring down at her shoes, blocking the light. Christine hadn't realized the homeowner had any kids in the house. That probably went a long way towards explaining the footsteps and missing keys.

"Is your dad still on the phone?" She asked the silent girl.

Slowly the girl raised her face to look at Christine but, as her yellow hair parted around her face, Christine was startled to see that the girl had no features, no eyes, nose, or mouth. Her face was simply an indistinct blur, and Christine realized she could see the pattern of the green wallpaper through the girl's body.

Slowly, the girl raised her arms toward Christine, as if she were silently pleading to be picked up. Christine took a shaky step back on the stairs and nearly lost her footing. She looked behind herself to find steady footing on the next lowest stair. When she turned back, the figure of the little girl was gone as if it had never been there.

Before she could even comprehend what she was seeing, she was hit with a wintry blast of air. The wave passed over her and through her. When she turned, she realized she could follow its course through the dark basement. It was a faintly luminescent yellow-green glow that moved quickly through the basement gloom before hitting, and presumably passing through, the concrete wall.

Christine stared dumbly down at her hands, still clutching the recording device and camera, both turned off. For a moment she felt a stab of regret. Why hadn't she gotten the encounter on tape?! But just as quickly she realized it didn't matter. She'd never started ghost hunting to prove anything to anyone other then herself. And she'd just gotten the proof that she'd always wanted. Unlike the things she had seen when out with her ghost-hunting group Christine didn't doubt for a minute that what she had seen and felt was real.

Christine made a hasty goodbye to the homeowner, not even trying to explain to him what she had just seen and felt. She would never go ghost hunting again, but she had a new found respect for the people who would, in passing, tell her a story about the haunted house they had once lived in.

The Portsmouth Music Hall has been the site of several strange happenings throughout its history. People are rarely surprised to find that it is haunted, knowing of its unusual history.

The Music Hall in Portsmouth has the type of long convoluted history you'd expect of a 120-year-old theater that was built at the site of not just the first poor house in the United States, but also a prison, a Baptist meeting house, and auditorium—and also the site of a segregated "colored" burying ground. With a past like that, it's no wonder the Music Hall is haunted!

In its earliest incarnation, the location where the Music Hall now stands was shared by a prison and one of six almshouses that stood in Portsmouth at the time. The almshouse had two rather notable residents. The first was Molly Bridget, a renowned fortune teller, who lived in the almshouse in 1782. A local farmer, trying to prove that Molly had bewitched his pigs cut the ears off of the animals and burned them in a fire. At the same time the sows ears were burning, Molly flung herself from her room at the almshouse and started to frantically run from room to room before finally bursting into flames. Convinced of her crimes, the other residents at the almshouse buried her body in an unmarked grave near the almshouse. As she was buried, a great storm came in from the sea, further convincing the terrified residents that they had cast a witch from their midst.

The almshouse was destroyed in the Great Fire of 1813. Ironically enough, forty years after the fire ravaged Portsmouth, it was discovered to have been set by a resident of the very almshouse that was destroyed by it. Miss Colbath, who was later discovered to have been the cause of the blaze, had moved into the almshouse after her employer had fired her for visiting male guests at night alone in their rooms at the Inn where she was a maid. Miss Colbath

The Portsmouth Music Hall is an important landmark in a city known for its history and culture.

swore as she left her former place of employment that she'd burn the place down, and a few days later, that's precisely what she did. Along with the Inn, over one hundred shops, sixty-four homes, and three dozen barns were destroyed in the blaze.

This was only one of several fires that took place in this area of Portsmouth. Later on, a Baptist meeting house and an auditorium replaced the almshouse and prison. They too would burn down in a massive fire that would destroy much the neighborhood around them.

It was not until 1878 that the building we now think of as the Music Hall was built on the location on Chestnut Street. The Music Hall opened its doors, reportedly big enough to allow elephants and horses to have access to the stage, to a sold-out comedy show. The Music Hall thrived until 1926, when competition forced it to close its doors.

In 1946, the Music Hall was reopened, and was again an important part of the arts in Portsmouth, though it caused more then a little scandal when it decided to show the film Reefer Madness in 1947. The theater would thrive for twenty-five years before being bought and closed by E.M. Lowe in an attempt to keep it from competing with The Colonial Theater.

It was not until 1987 that the theater was finally reopened again and restored to its former glory. Today, this 900-seat theater is the premier performing arts center in New Hampshire. It is the oldest theater in the state and the second oldest in New England. It was not until this latest reincarnation of the Music Hall that stories began to circulate about the "phantom" of the theater.

Stories about the phantom vary. Some people think that there are as many as three ghosts, one of them the spirit of a former stage hand that haunts the theater. Others say that the Music Hall is plagued by a poltergeist and not a ghost at all. Others are equally as firm that there is one, and only, one phantom. No other ghosts need apply.

Many of the strange events occur outside the box office in the lobby. There is an eerie feeling of being watched when no one is there, of walking into cold spots, or even being gripped with an icy hand. Several people had reported experiences beyond just being grabbed. A few swear they were held paralyzed, unable to move or even to speak or alert anyone around them to their discomfort, for up to several minutes at a time. Patrons inside the Music Hall have complained of a person blocking their view, when later it is

The Music Hall was built with enormous backdoors so horses and elephants could be brought onstage. Less than fifty years later it would close.

discovered the seat in front of them has been empty during the entire performance. These shadowy figures can be seen outlined along the theater's walls as though patrons are making their way to their seats even when the theater is empty or everyone is already sitting down. It cannot be a simple trick of the lights because the human-shaped shadows are very distinct and they move from place to place just as the shadows of a real person moving around the theater would.

Often, when no one is on stage, workers see the curtain ripple as though there is someone walking behind it, dragging a hand along the inside. The phantom most often manifests itself by sound. He or she is most often heard nervously shuffling their invisible feet back and forth restlessly. The lights on stage and the chandeliers hanging above the crowd sometimes swing back and forth by themselves.

One visitor to the Music Hall got up close and personal with a ghost in nineteenth-century garb. When this theater goer noticed the figure standing by the stairs in the lobby, she assumed it was an actor, under hire to add an authentic Victorian air to the Hall, dressed in period costume. When she walked up to tell them what a great job they were doing, the '"actor" disappeared in front of her eyes. It is thought that it is this ghost who is heard walking up and down the Music Halls grand staircase during performances. At the top of these same stairs is a very large cold spot that has given more then one theater goer a chill. This cold sport is stationary and quite dense. It is said that you can easily feel along the edges of where the cold spot ends and meets the regularly air flow around it, which discounts it being simply because of overactive air conditioning.

The Music Hall maintains the old tradition of keeping a "ghost light" burning onstage, which is a single lamp lit in the middle of the stage when performances aren't going on. Ostensibly, this is to ward off unwanted spirits, who have long been rumored to be drawn to theaters. But the ghost light serves the far more practical service of making sure that no one who is lost and wandering around backstage can fall off the edge of the stage unknowingly, landing in the orchestra pit. So far the ghost light doesn't seem to be working too well in regards to keeping the spirits away, but that may be because the Phantom is hardly an unwanted addition to the staff. The phantom hasn't scared anyone yet and adds a bit of quirky class to the Music Hall.

Chase Home for Children

A 19ᵗʰ Century Orphanage, Located on Middle Street

The Chase Home for Children, which is not to be confused with Chase House located at the Strawbery Banke Museum, is the place that creators of urban legends dream of. It is big, it is old, it has a shadowy history dating back to times when records were not well kept and cruelties were commonplace facts of life. So, not surprisingly, there are some over-the-top legends associated with this former home for orphaned and troubled children.

The Chase Home for Children is located on Middle Street at the end of a long twisty driveway that snakes through the overgrowth. Stories about the supposedly haunted house are over the top but one look at the building makes a believer out of many skeptics.

Of course, the downside to all the myth is that few, if any, facts are verifiable and it is near impossible for the serious ghost hunter to sort out what might be true, what might be a little bit true, and what is entirely false. Everyone is so sure that Chase Home is haunted that no one really bothers to check and see if it really is as haunted as the stories say it is. The building, a stately old brick estate, set deep back in the woods and covered with ivy, certainly looks as if it must be haunted. It also has the sort of history that seems common to haunted houses around New England.

Built in 1807, by 1871, Chase Home was established as a home for orphaned children. Since then it has always been used, one way or another, as an orphanage or court-appointed children's home. It has seen its share of troubled children over the years. One of these troubled children, legend tells us, hung herself in the dormitory she shared with several other girls. The ghostly figure of this young girl still roams the hallways of the Chase Home for Children. When she is spotted, she runs away from witnesses before disappearing through a wall.

This girl may, or may not be, the source of the girlish screams that echo through the hallways at night. The bloodcurdling screams are unmistakably that of a young girl crying out in fright, pain, or both. More mundane manifestations at the Chase Home for Children include doors that won't stay locked, or closed, even when the keys are all accounted for, and light switches that have the irritating habit of flipping on and off by themselves.

The kitchen seems to be particularly haunted. It too is plagued with electrical problems and unstable locked doors. On top of this, the large kitchen fan used to suck heat and smells from the room acts erratically, switching itself on and off at random. Various kitchen personnel have described everything from smelling things that weren't there to cabinet doors that have a habit of swinging open just in time for unwary cooks to walk straight into them. One thing is for certain, the kitchen ghost likes to keep everyone on their toes.

The vacant third floor seems to be trying to give the kitchen a run for its money when it comes to the title of "most haunted." Originally, the third floor was home to counselors at the Chase Home for Children. Today, it is empty of rooms and used as storage space. From the second floor, you can hear footsteps pacing restlessly at night and sometimes it sounds as if many people are walking at once.

The Salon Spirits
A Brand New Shopping Plaza Haunted

Crystal thought the job at the new hair salon was a dream come true. She had just received her beauticians license when she got the offer to work in a beautiful brand-new building in a salon that offered the most up-to-date and modern appliances available. Most of the girls Crystal had gone to beauty school with were still looking for work and the ones who had found jobs were acting as receptionists and sweeping up hair in second-rate salons. No one that Crystal knew had gotten an offer like the one she had just accepted.

The grand opening of the salon came and went in a blur. Crystal quickly fell into the routine at the new hair salon. She really liked the girls she was working with and the clients were fun. She didn't get to do as much haircutting as she'd like; usually the receptionist scheduled her with waxing and nail appointments. But at least she wasn't answering phones and spending the whole day with a broom in her hand while she watched other employees interact with the clients.

The one thing that did surprise Crystal was how shoddy the building really was for being brand-new construction. The lights flickered sometimes and she worried what would happen if they went out entirely. The other girls said it was because the fuses couldn't handle all the hairdryers and things going on at once, but Crystal noticed that the lights flickered most often at night when she was alone counting the cash register drawer and cleaning up. It didn't seem to happen during the day when there were all kinds of electrical appliances going.

The other thing that surprised Crystal was how messy some of the other girls could be. Every time she walked into the back supply room where they mixed the dyes for customers coloring their hair, she had to step over a big puddle of water. It made no sense to her. There was no reason for anyone to be using water right in front of the door and the sink was all the way over on the other side of the room. She'd looked around for leaks, not wanting to accuse anyone of a mess that wasn't their fault, but she could never find the source of the liquid. The walls and ceiling were all totally unmarked, nothing showed the telltale ring of wetness she would expect if a pipe were leaking and dripping in the walls.

The other girls didn't seem to like the job as much as Crystal. They were quitting left and right. Crystal figured that the beauty business just had a high turn over and didn't think much of it until word started to go around about the reasons the girls who were quitting were giving as their reason for leaving. One girl said she got blinding headaches as soon as she walked into the building. Crystal would have just passed it off as a bad reaction to the chemical smells hairdressers dealt with on a daily basis, but the woman who made the complaint had been working in salons for twenty-five years! If anyone should be accustomed to the smell of relaxer and hair dye, it would have been her. Another women left because she said she hadn't been able to sleep at night ever since she started the job and another left right after that because she said, of all the things, that she had nightmares about the building.

Crystal herself hadn't had any sleepless nights or nightmares or headaches, but sometimes, at night when the lights began to flicker, she felt as though there was someone in the room with her though she was alone. Sometimes it felt as though there was someone standing directly behind her! Within a few weeks, Crystal started to dread the nights she'd see her name on the schedule to close, especially the week nights when they stayed at the salon late and only a few girls were working.

It was one of those quiet weeknights at closing that Crystal first really started to realize that something was wrong in a truly unexplainable way. She had just finished sweeping and mopping all of the floors for the evening when the lights began to flicker worse than they ever had before. She held her breath for a minute, sure that the lights were really going to go out this time. They flickered another half a dozen times and then came on strong, humming gently in the closed shop. Crystal breathed a sigh of relief.

That's when the lights flicked out, plunging the salon into darkness.

Crystal took a stumbling step forward, automatically searching for the light switch next to the door, even though if she had stopped to think about it, she would have realized the light wasn't going to come on with the flick of a switch. She took a few shambling steps forward and heard a slosh of liquid. Her teeth began chattering uncontrollably as the liquid seeped through her shoes. It was unbelievably cold!

Crystal was so surprised she fell a little, but before she could hit the ground she felt strong hands grab her around the middle and pull her back up onto her feet... She whirled around in surprise and flailed her arms around wildly trying to connect with whoever was in the small back supply room with her, but there was no one there. In one of the distant rooms of the salon she heard someone begin to scream.

Thankfully at that moment the lights came back on. Crystal took one wild look around the back supply room, but her eyes told her what she already knew. She was alone in the room. And even though she had just finished mopping the floor herself before the lights went out, there was an enormous puddle of water just in front of the door, same as always. After one last look around the room, she took off at a run to see what all the screaming was about.

Crystal followed the screams to a small coat closest near the front desk where clients left their purses and coats when they came in for a haircut or color. Hesitantly, she went to open it and was surprised to find it was locked. They rarely locked the door, only when a client requested it to keep their purse and shopping bags secure, and tonight Crystal was the only person who had the key needed to lock the door. As she slid the key into the lock, she had the irrational fear that it simply wasn't going to work and that the other girl would be stuck in there until they could get a locksmith to come in.

But the key turned easily in the lock and the other girl flew out of the closest as though it had exploded. She was yelling and screaming but it wasn't until she slapped Crystal hard in the shoulder that she realized the girl was mad at her.

"Do you think that was funny?" the other woman yelled. "I could kill you! I'm telling the owner about this."

Crystal stammered out that it wasn't her fault and tried to explain that she had been clear on the other side of the building when the lights went out, but the other girl was having none of it.

"Oh yeah," she snapped, pulling up the sleeve of her button down smock. "I guess I did this to myself."

Clearly marked on the woman's pale skin was a row of bruises perfectly shaped as though someone had grabbed her roughly by the arms and pushed her back into the closest before locking it. Crystal started to say that was impossible, but then she remembered the rough hands that had grabbed her when she began to fall.

The next day the owner came in but she was too busy to listen to any stories about the night before from either Crystal or the other employee. The owner walked in with a plumber, an electrician, and the man who owned the entire shopping plaza. Crystal was out back mixing hair dye for another colorist when the group trooped back there.

"And here," exclaimed the salon owner, "this is where we always find a big puddle of water. It's freezing cold, too. It must be leaking from the central air or something."

"No way," said the plaza owner, shaking his head emphatically. "You have this room subdivided out special, remember? There are no pipes or ductwork in this room. If anything is leaking, it must be something you brought in."

Crystal spoke up, telling them about the lights going out the night before, but she was cut off quickly. The same thing had happened to a few other people at the shop and they already knew all about it. The electrician and the plumber went over the whole shop and found nothing amiss. They moved on to the other units in the plaza, but not only did they find nothing wrong, but none of the other tenants complained of any problems. None of the electrical problems happened while the plaza owner was there with the electricians and no pooled water appeared in the backroom like it usually did. That night Crystal closed and everything was perfectly, and thankfully, normal.

But Crystal couldn't forget about the row of fingerprints bruised into her co-worker's arm. Even though she knew she would miss the girls she worked with, she began searching for a new job. Like so many others before her, Crystal was ready to leave rather than take the chance of running into something spooky again. As word got around that she was looking for a new job, other employees started coming to her talking about their experiences. A few showed her bruises that were startlingly like the other ones she had seen the night of her own odd encounter.

Plenty of the other girls told her stories, though, that didn't end with them being shoved or bruised. One girl said if she was in the backroom and couldn't find something she needed, she would just politely ask out loud for it and usually when she turned around, she'd find it on the work bench, put in plain view. Another girl, like Crystal, had started to fall one night and had been caught before she hit the ground. As the workers became more open about the inexplicable things they had experienced, they realized that the salon must be haunted by two very different sprits. One was a helpful ghost who didn't want to see them hurt, and who left behind a puddle of water in his wake, for reasons they couldn't even begin to guess. The other spirit was angry and liked to stay up front near the front desk and the nearby closet that locked from the outside.

After talking it out, the girls decided to look into the history of the plaza and to take what precautions they could against the angry ghost in the front of the building. After closing one night they replaced the closets handle with a new doorknob—one that couldn't be locked. One of the girls said her Grandmother swore that carrying salt in your pocket kept dark spirits at bay and even though everyone scoffed when she said this, within a week's time, when the girls were closing for the night, most of them had a small baggie in their pants pocket with a little twist of salt in it. No one could really say for sure if the salt worked, but no one with salt on their person ever had a strange experience with the ghost in the front lobby again.

Trying to find a reason for their strange patrons was decidedly harder then taking precautions against them. The plaza was brand new. No workers, as far as their newspaper research could tell them, had died while working on the structure. They thought maybe the site of the plaza had once been an old house or graveyard, but before being a plaza, it had been an old parking garage and before that a small park. They couldn't seem to find a traumatic death or accident in the area no matter how far back they looked.

In the end, the haunting would remain a mystery. No reason was found for it. The workers sometimes still found puddles of water in the back room but the angry spirit up front who had frightened so many of them was silenced, possibly by the salt, possibly because one brave girl had worked up the courage one night to ask it to leave. Even so, when Crystal got an offer to go and cut hair somewhere else, she took it. If two ghosts could wander in and set up shop in the salon, then who was to say that in the future there wouldn't be more?

Fort Constitution State Park

The Portsmouth Lighthouse, the Light Keeper's House, and Fort Constitution

The Light and the Keeper's House

The Portsmouth Harbor Lighthouse stands sentry over Portsmouth Harbor. It is one of only eleven remaining lighthouses that were built in the United States before the American Revolution and it is the oldest lighthouse north of Boston. In 1771, the first lighthouse was built at this location, though the one that stands on New Castle today was erected in 1878. This forty-eight-foot-high tower was one of the first "cast iron" lighthouses built in New England and is one of the few remaining of this style to be seen in the area.

You can't talk about the Portsmouth Harbor Lighthouse without talking about the two people who loved it the most—Joshua Card and Connie Scovill Small. Joshua Card held the post of lighthouse keeper at Portsmouth Harbor longer then anyone else. In 1905 he retired, at the ripe old age of eighty-five, after thirty-five years served at Portsmouth Harbor Lighthouse. He was known for his military precision and for the large letter "K" pinned to his jacket. The "K," he jokingly told people, referred to him as "Kaptain" of the light.

In life, Connie Small was called "the first lady of the light." Over the course of nearly thirty years, she and her husband, the lighthouse keeper Elson Small, lived at no less then a half a dozen different lighthouse up and down the New England coast before moving to the Portsmouth Harbor Lighthouse. Connie's job at the lighthouse was to fly signal flags from the top to warn sailors of coming storms. She made quilts from the damaged and discarded flags that she gave to friends. Late in her life, she wrote a book called The Lighthouse Keepers Wife, chronicling her years at various lighthouses. Connie Small passed away in 2005, a staggering 103 years old.

Both Connie Smalls and Joshua Cards ghosts are thought to still reside in the lighthouse that was so important to them in life, along with a slew of other spirits. In 2000, the lighthouse was leased to the American Lighthouse Foundation for upkeep. While repainting the inside of the tower around the stairs, a few members of the Foundation very distinctly heard a man's voice speaking to them, although the words came out so rushed, the

The Portsmouth Harbor Lighthouse is part of the Fort Constitution Historic Site. It has been the scene of several paranormal happenings over the years.

meaning couldn't be discerned. Previously, a lighthouse keeper's wife had reported the very same phenomena, which she had experienced while removing Christmas decorations in the same spot on the stairs.

The Coast Guard, who was responsible for the keeping of the light when it became automated in the 1960s, were not surprised to hear this particular ghost story. They had several different ghostly encounters in the forty years they'd been keepers of the light. One night, while monitoring the lighthouse, several of the Coast Guardsmen saw a woman in a long white dress exit the structure and walk along the seawall. They rushed out to tell the woman she was trespassing, but could find no one there. The guards left in the control room could still see the lady on their monitors—even as their colleagues were radioing back to say the spot was deserted.

Later, the Coast Guard saw footprints belonging to both an adult and child appear in the dew in the middle of a helicopter launch pad near the lighthouse. The footprints trailed out to the sea and stayed for several days on the asphalt. There are many Coast Guard reports of shadowy figures moving around in the Portsmouth Harbor Light and the lighthouse keeper's house, that stands nearby, at night when they know the buildings are supposed to be empty. On all of these occasions, whomever was sent to investigate never found a living person to blame the sightings upon.

Both the History Channel and the New England Ghost Project have investigated the Portsmouth Harbor Lighthouse. Both groups brought psychics to the tower and told them nothing of the lighthouse's history. John Holland, the psychic who was at the lighthouse taping an episode of Psychic History for the History Channel, encountered what he described as an "old sea captain" standing on the stairs near a window overlooking the ocean. It was at precisely the spot where people had so often heard a man's voice talking to them. Chillingly, Holland, said the ghost had a large letter "K" prominently pinned to the front of his coat! It was only later that anyone told him the history of the light and the significance of the man with the large letter "K."

In the lighthouse keeper's home, now converted to offices for the Coast Guard, the psychic working with the New England Ghost Project said she clearly saw the spirit of a woman walking through the rooms. In her hands, this spirit was clutching a bouquet of flowers similar to the ones that Connie Small had been buried with. Many people feel it is only fitting that Connie Small's ghost should haunt the old house. At the time the psychic first encountered it, talk had already begun about turning the structure into a museum and naming it after the woman known as the "First lady of the light."

The Fort

The Portsmouth Harbor Lighthouse and the lighthouse keeper's house are only part of the attractions at Fort Constitution State Park. In the same complex visitors can also tour the fort itself. A fort has stood at this site at the mouth of the Piscataqua River and Portsmouth Harbor as far back as 1632, when it was called Fort William and Mary. In 1774, when Paul Revere gave warning that the British were coming, Portsmouth residents stormed their own fort to seize gunpowder and weapons in order to protect the city and to keep those valuable resources from falling into enemy hands.

The Fort was renamed Fort Constitution in the 1800s after it was expanded extensively. In 1973, it became listed in the National Register of Historic Places and was opened to the public.

The worst bloodshed ever witnessed at the fort was not an act of war, but one of tragedy. In 1809, a large Independence Day celebration was thrown at the fort. An errant spark accidentally set off a reported 300 pounds of gunpowder, which set off an unimaginable number of cannonballs at the same time. There were nine deaths, both civilian and military, and hundreds of injuries.

At least one of Fort Constitution's ghosts seems to be linked to this great tragedy. Wandering around the fort, this spirit is wracked with guilt and refuses to leave. Psychics say the ghost is filled with remorse and doesn't understand why it survived an accident that hurt so many others. Because the spirit is so sure that it can never make amends for the accident it caused, it is punishing itself by walking the grounds forever. No one is exactly sure who this ghost may have been or why it feels responsible for the tragedy that was, by all historic accounts that we have found, truly just a terrible accident.

Within the sentry room and watchtower of Fort Constitution another ghost walks. Most often, it manifests itself simply through the heavy sound of its work-boot clad footsteps walking up and down the tower stairs, although some people claim to have seen the figure of a man materialize out of thin air in front of them. All activity from this spirit happens only during the dead of night. During daylight hours, not a single ghostly event has been reported in this part of the fort.

At Fort Constitution, the oldest remaining structure is a relatively small space measuring twelve feet square. It was originally a gun

Fort Constitution is open to the public, despite still being part of an active Coast Guard station. Both visitors and employees of the historic site sometimes come head to head with the unearthly.

powder room at Fort William and Mary. People flat out just do not like being near this space—even if they cannot give a tangible reason as to why. Some pictures taken of the area have yielded unusual spirit photographs. Rather then showing the orb photos that are so common in spirit photography, pictures of this room show vivid yellow and green streaks of light.

But the strangest incidence at Fort Constitution is surely that of the odd footprints that disappeared just as suddenly as they appeared one day. On an otherwise normal day at the Fort, the Coast Guard happened upon some strange looking footprints in the parking lot. They were described as looking dark and almost oily. They began without lead up in the middle of the parking lot and continued on several feet. The Coastguard then found a much smaller pair of footprints, also strangely dark and oily, that started up at the other side of the parking lot. The two sets of footprints walked up to each other and ended just as abruptly, and unexplainably, as they had started. It was as though two different people, a child and an adult, had been dropped into the middle of the parking lot from above, walked about a few feet, and then were plucked back into the sky.

Curious, a few Coast Guardsmen tried feeling the footprints to see if they could identify the substance that made them look so strange. No matter how hard they rubbed, they couldn't seem to get any of the material up to investigate it. The footprints remained for several days, unfading, until all of a sudden, they were gone, as if they had never been there in the first place. No amount of water or scrubbing could mar them when the men tried and no one could figure out how they could be so quickly gone without a trace. The phenomenon has not been repeated again. At least not yet.

South Cemetery

A Collection of Five Burying Grounds— the Sites of the Last Executions in the State

South Cemetery is something of a misnomer—technically, there is no South Cemetery at all. Instead of being a specific place, it is the name given to a collection of several smaller cemeteries in Portsmouth. Ask a local where South Cemetery is and you may get a patronizing smile along with your directions, or you may hear the quip that any cemetery except North Cemetery is "South." The five cemeteries that make up South Cemetery are Auburn Cemetery, Cotton's Cemetery, Harmony Grove Cemetery, Proprietors' Burying Ground, and Sagamore Cemetery. The first of the five was begun as far back as 1671, and many of the old tombstones can still be seen today, jostling for place with modern-day gravestones.

South Cemetery is a collection of several smaller cemeteries where modern tombstones lay side by side with ancient ones. Many of the spirits here are restless ones.

Semantics and geography aside, the thing that most differentiates these burial grounds from North Cemetery is how well they are tended. Come by any one of these cemeteries on a nice summer day and you're likely to see more joggers and Frisbee players then you'll see mourners. It is an unlikely setting for a long history of executions, death, and ghosts.

The Execution of Ruth Blay

In 1768, the city of Portsmouth was rocked by news of a scandal. It was discovered that Ruth Blay, an unmarried twenty-five-year-old teacher, had buried the body of her illegitimate baby under the floorboards of the very schoolhouse she taught at. Ruth said the child was stillborn, though the medical examiners of the time couldn't tell if the child had been born dead or alive, neither could they tell if the child had been murdered.

During this time period there were more than 600 crimes in New Hampshire that merited the death penalty. So, in the end, it made no difference if the child had been born alive or dead. Concealing the death of an illegitimate child was illegal in and of itself in the 1700s. A mere twenty-nine years earlier, two other women, Sarah Simpson and Penelope Kenny, had been executed in Portsmouth for the very same crime. Like Simpson and Kenny, Ruth Blay was sentenced to hang.

Surprisingly, public sentiment was with the young school teacher and the ruling was viciously unpopular in the city. For months, appeals dragged on, but one by one, they were all shot down. The sentence stood.

On the day the execution was to take place, thousands of people in and around Portsmouth came to watch the hanging. Ruth Play was brought by cart to the gallows. One witness to the execution described the sound of her shrieking filling the air. Ruth Play was so wretched a figure that even those who had come to see her hang started to call for her to be let go.

According to legend and to some old newspaper accounts, as the clock ticked down to hanging time, the Governor did issue a reprieve to the young school teacher. But in a final twist of fate it did not reach her in time. Despite hearing that the Governor was reconsidering the matter, Sheriff Thomas Packer, who wanted to get things over with so as to not delay his supper, hung Ruth Blay as quickly as possible.

The crowd, furious at the Sheriff, would later hang him in effigy. But, of course, what was done could not be undone. Ruth Blay was still just as dead. It was the last execution to take place in the state of New Hampshire.

The gallows themselves had been constructed in a northwest corner of what is today South Cemetery. A row of tombstones covers the spot today. The body of Ruth Blay was taken down from where it hung and was buried in an unmarked grave somewhere in the area that cemetery now covers.

Perhaps because of the way she was wronged in life or because of the further insult of being buried in an unmarked grave, the ghost of Ruth Play is supposed to roam South Cemetery. She is most often felt in the area around the South Street entrance to the burying grounds. Visitors report feeling as though something cold is plucking at their clothing, almost as if trying to lead them somewhere, or to keep them from going away from a certain spot.

Other Strange Phenomena

Like Point of Graves Cemetery, South Cemetery also has some glowing tombstones. In the case of South Cemetery, there are two tombstones, standing side by side and dating from 1873, that are said to glow late at night. The odd illumination has even been caught on film, though skeptics pass the phenomena off on the usual, either glare from a streetlamp or a full moon.

Furthermore, sometimes a dark female shape is seen lingering around the site of the glowing gravestones. She is said to whisper something indecipherable to herself while ringing her hands and pacing back and forth. This has lead some people to question whether the two graves may have been inadvertently buried on top of the unmarked resting spot of Ruth Blay.

However, the two tombstones have a separate, though equally dark, history of their own. Far from hiding the secret resting spot of Ruth Blay, they are the tombstones of two women who were rather famously murdered on the nearby Isles of Shoals. The ghost of the ladies' murderer is said to still visit the scene of the grisly murder (of which more can be read in the upcoming chapter, "The Haunted Islands of New Hampshire"). It has been surmised that the lady ghost haunts her final resting place rather than the place she called home because of the lingering ghostly presence of the man who killed her.

Why only one of the murder victims has been seen is unexplained and probably unexplainable though there is nothing to say that the ghost of the other woman doesn't manifest itself in more subtle ways.

Perhaps one is the woman seen standing at the tombstone while the other causes the glow.

South Cemetery is a must-see spot for those interested in ghost photography. While of course there is no such thing as a guaranteed ghost photography spot and spirits are notoriously poor at playing to an expectant audience, many of the local ghost hunters say this is the place to bring your camera if you want the chance to get your own ghostly souvenir.

On the eastern side of the cemetery, near Clough Drive, there is a small cache of tombstones just outside the graveyards walls. This is the number one spot in the cemetery to try your hand at spirit photography, though the area right near the South Street entrance is a close number two.

Where There's Smoke, There's Fire
A Loyal Dog Keeps Watch Over His Master—Even After Death

Some people would have found the house on the small side but, considering it was just a mid-twenties architect and her beagle living there, Sarah found it to be more cozy than cramped. Honestly, the new house was a dream come true for the young woman. It was a beautifully renovated carriage house, dating from the 1800s, with hardwood floors, federal-style brick walls, and exposed wood beams in the enormous sunken living room. The previous owners had put skylights throughout the 1,200 square-foot one-bedroom house, making it a bright happy place to curl up in a reading chair, entertain friends, or sit back to enjoy the wood stove. Sarah had never thought she'd be able to afford to own her own home and was amazed at the incredible price she'd gotten on the building. It was precisely the type of place that Sarah would have designed herself; it blended in perfectly with the historic neighborhood surrounding it, and combined modern conveniences with all the little historical details that gave a home character.

Sarah's roommate, and best friend, Gus the beagle, seemed as happy with their new home as she was. As soon as Sarah had signed the papers for the place, she moved Gus right in. The pudgy black, tan, and white dog ran directly into the living room and curled up next to the white enameled woodstove as if he had lived there his entire life. It instantly became his favorite spot in the house. By the time Sarah had unpacked his well-loved L.L. Bean dog bed, she already knew exactly where he wanted it.

The two old friends fell into an easy rhythm, quickly making the house their home. Every day as Sarah walked up the cobblestone pathway to her front door, Gus would run up to greet her and she'd think again how lucky they were and what a find the old carriage house had been for them.

After a few weeks in the new house, Sarah awoke to frantic howls coming from the beagle's favorite spot in the living room. Gus never barked. Frantic, Sarah pulled on a robe and ran out to see what was wrong. Shaking with fear in his bright plaid bed, Gus barked uneasily a few times. Fainter, but definitely there, Sarah heard another dog answer as if from far away. Suddenly, she relaxed. Gus was just upset because he heard a neighbor's dog barking, she thought. Glancing at the hallway clock she saw it was just after five in the morning. Deciding it didn't make much sense to go back to bed when she had to be awake in less than two hours anyway, Sarah headed off into the kitchen to make herself a cup of coffee.

"C'mon, Gus!" she called, clapping her hands.

Sarah opened up the kitchen door to let Gus outside and was surprised when she didn't see his roly-poly form dash out into the small backyard. She turned, called again, and got no answer. Walking back into the living room, she found the dog rooted in the same spot, still as a statue. Unnerved, she reached down to nudge him into moving but before her hand could touch him, the normally good-natured dog bared his teeth and jumped up to snap at her.

Sarah gave a yelp and snatched her hand away. Now she was worried. Gus never snapped at anyone. He was the kindest, most passive dog Sarah had ever seen. In the distance, the other dog barked twice and fell silent. Gus gave himself a shake and hopped out of bed as if nothing was the matter. He ran up to the kitchen door, for all appearances his usual happy self, and looked back at Sarah as if asking what was wrong with her.

Oh, well, though Sarah, we all have our bad days. I guess Gus woke up on the wrong side of the doggy bed today.

She was nervous that evening as she came up her front walk. Would Gus be his usual self? Would he try to bite her again? Maybe he was sick and should go to the vet? Putting her key into the lock and opening the door, she forgot her worries about the incident with the dog that morning. The house was filled with smoke!

Sarah rushed from room to room looking for the cause of the thick smoke that filled the house. The gas fireplace was off. She hadn't left the stove on. In the end, she couldn't find the source of the gray haze that filled the entire house. Coughing a little, she opened up some windows and almost instantly, the house was clear, leaving just a lingering smell of a fire she couldn't find. As the last wafts of smoke faded, Sarah noticed Gus fast asleep in his spot, unconcerned by either the smoke or her running around the house.

Afraid that old wiring was the cause of the mysterious fire, Sarah called in an electrician. After hearing the story, the man went over the houses wiring very carefully but told her there was no way the wiring should cause her concern. It all looked to have been replaced fairly recently and was in perfect condition.

Sarah never did find any trace of a fire. Some afternoons when she came home from work, she would think she caught the scent of smoke in the still air of the old carriage house, but other afternoons there was nothing; the air was clean and fresh.

But the smoke was the least of her concerns. Sarah wasn't getting much sleep. More mornings than not, she was awoken by Gus barking back and forth with the distant dog, and several mornings she woke up with her beloved beagle pulling restlessly at the pant leg of her pajamas, as though trying to hurry her from her bed.

No amount of scolding could get Gus to leave her alone when these moods struck him. He worried at her unceasingly, not calming down until she was up out of bed and on her way. Sarah didn't know what to do but to get a dog crate and start making him sleep locked up at night so she could get a full-night's rest. Sad at the idea, but knowing it was for the best, Sarah walked down to the local pet store to buy a crate.

Walking up the street, one of Sarah's older neighbors invited her in for a cup of tea. Sarah, wanting to be polite and wanting to put off the unhappy errand took her up on the offer. The two women chit chatted for awhile about the neighborhood. Sarah was asked how she liked the area.

"Oh, I know I shouldn't complain since I have a dog myself and know what it's like," she replied, "but when that neighbor's dog gets going in the morning, it starts my dog Gus barking, too. I barely get a wink of sleep. I guess they must have to leave for work earlier than I, but five in the morning seems pretty early to have your dog out in the yard waking up the whole neighborhood."

The old woman was puzzled. "I know every neighbor on this block. The only one I know of with a dog is you, dear."

Then the old woman seemed to hesitate a moment. She eyed Sarah in a speculative way and seemed to reach some sort of decision with herself.

"You ever smell smoke in that little house of yours?" she asked quietly.

Sarah was stunned. She stuttered out the entire story, the smoke-filled house and the problems with Gus. The neighbor nodded knowingly as she talked. When Sarah finally stopped for a breath, the woman broke in, patting her hand, and refilling her mug of tea.

"I almost didn't say anything," the old woman told her. "I've seen quite a few people come and go from your house in my life and whenever I see a dog move in there, I know what's coming. Back in the 1813, just after the original carriage house was built on the site where your house stands today, a great fire ripped through this part of Portsmouth. When it was all said and done, more than 200 buildings were lost in that blaze. The carriage house was one of them. When they were shifting through the ashes, they found the body of a young girl in the wreckage. Looks like she had rushed in trying to save the horses. She had a little dog that followed her everywhere she went. When they brought her body out for burial, the legend goes that the dog stayed right by it. They say the poor thing pined away for his mistress and followed her into the afterlife soon after. In time, a new carriage house was built right over the ruins of the old one, and even longer after that, carriage houses became obsolete. Some were torn down, some, like your house, found new uses. Whenever someone moves into your house and brings a dog with them, they say they smell smoke and hear a dog barking out to theirs in the night. Now, I don't know how much you believe in this stuff, but I think that what you and Gus are hearing is that little girl's dog, telling your Gus to watch out for you."

Sarah didn't know what to think. She wasn't even sure if she believed in ghosts to begin with. Ghost dogs seemed even more unlikely. She smiled politely at the old woman and made some sort of non-committal response to close the conversation.

But when she came home later that night, sans dog crate, she suddenly realized that she believed the story. When Gus woke her up the next morning she got up uncomplainingly. Hearing the near indiscernible barks coming from far away she walked out into the backyard and listened carefully. She couldn't tell where it sounded like the yelps were coming from. Inside, they sounded slightly louder than they had outside and as she walked from room to room, Gus fast on her heels, she realized that the noise was coming from the thin air all around her.

Strawbery Banke

Portsmouth's Oldest Neighborhood and Some of Its Oldest Ghosts
Located on Marcy Street

*The Strawbery Banke Museum is open daily, May 1st through
December 30th.*

In 1630, when Captain Walter Neal first sailed up the Piscataqua
River looking for a likely spot to start a new settlement, he was
much impressed by the wild growth of strawberries found on
one sunny bank of the river. He was so impressed, in fact, that he
decided to name his burgeoning settlement after the small red
fruit. The settlers, led by Captain Neal, were a group of London
Merchants calling themselves the Laconia Company. However, the
Laconia Company would go bankrupt just eight short years later,
leaving the small town with no government charter and no legal
stability. It was not until the 1650s that the residents would petition
to rename the area Portsmouth and for it to become a city in its
own rights.

As time went on, and the city prospered, Portsmouth made a name
for itself worldwide as a port and ship-building town. Portsmouth
prospered but the area where the Laconia Company first raised
the city did not fare as well as the rest of the city. The beautiful
river bank covered in strawberries was long gone. In its place was
a run down ramshackle neighborhood known around town as the
"Puddle Docks." In time, the neighborhood only got worse with
many of the older houses knocked down to make way brickworks
factories, warehouses, and brothels. This south end neighborhood
of Portsmouth, containing some of the very first homes built in the
town, fell quickly into steep disrepair. It became an eclectic mix of
new tenement-style apartment buildings, more commonly called
plain old slums, and crumbling buildings ranging from the beginning
of Portsmouth's history to the unlovely, cheaply-made buildings of
the modern day.

In the early 1900s, some efforts were made to preserve this
historic area of Portsmouth. The Prescott heiresses, Josie and May,
started buying up old wharves along the waterfront and tearing
them down in a two-woman beautification process that resulted
in "Prescott Park," a well-kept grassy area that is still enjoyed by

Portsmouth residents today. But it was not until the 1960s, that Portsmouth residents as a whole really started to pay attention to the old Puddle Dock neighborhood. In an effort to restore their past, a group of concerned citizens drew up plans to recreate the old Strawbery Banke buildings. It was an idea that would eventually evolve into saving and restoring old buildings all throughout the seacoast area. The city granted this group nine and one half acres to achieve this end. They were able to save twenty-five houses. In a massive effort, the group picked over deteriorated houses throughout the city and surrounding area and had them moved to the nine-acre plot.

Today, the Strawbery Banke Museum neighborhood is a wonderful look into the history of early America. Guides dressed in period costumes talk about the ways of life throughout 400 years of American history. There are now more than thirty-five restored buildings on the nine and a half-acre plot, thirty of which are resting on their original foundations. The architecture shown at Strawbery Banke ranges from the 1600s all the way to the 1950s. Sometimes, the mix of time periods can be quite disconcerting! One half of Driscoe House at Strawbery Banke shows how the house looked in 1795 when it was used as a popular grains and feed store run by the Shapely family, and the other half shows a typical residential home of the 1950s.

Many of the houses at Strawbery Banke are reported to be haunted and visitors to the attraction have sometimes gotten up close and personal with some of these ghosts. Around the Halloween holiday season, there are many haunted tours and talks at Strawbery Banke about their more active ghosts.

Chase House

There is a lot of confusion over Chase House and the (possible) spirits that haunt it. It is well known that there is a very haunted Chase House in Portsmouth that was once used as a state-run home for orphans. Since Strawbery Banke's Chase House is quite famous, is located in the very haunted Strawbery Banke collection of buildings, and was also used as a home of orphans during one small part of its history, most people assume that it must be the famous haunted Chase House. However, the Chase House of ghostly legend is located on Middle Street (and more can be read about it in Chapter 16 of this book.) More than one

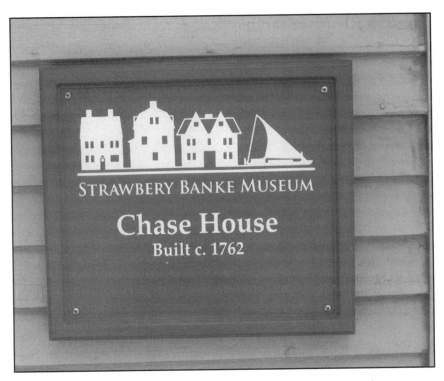

Despite the confusion over Portsmouth having two Chase Homes the one at Strawbery Banke Museum seems to be as haunted as the one located on Middle Street.

would-be "psychic" has walked into the Chase House at Strawbery Banke describing all the spirits of sad orphaned children there until it is, tactfully one hopes, pointed out to them that they are in the wrong house.

Despite the confusion of the two Chase House names, several of the Strawbery Banke volunteers have sworn that their Chase House is just as haunted as Portsmouth's other Chase House. At closing time they hear people walking around and talking softly but have never been able to find the source of the noise. One volunteer swore she felt some kind of demonic presence in the building and refused to be there alone, particularly at night.

Chase House was built in 1762 and stayed in the Chase family for many generations. The Chase family was made up of wealthy merchants and the beauty of Chase House reflects their money and social standing. It is probably one of the most accurately restored and decorated of Strawbery Banke's homes because the house remained

An exterior view of Strawbery Banke's Chase House. The restoration of what was once a wealthy merchant's private residence seems to have stirred up a few spirits.

in one family for so long and because they carefully recorded each item and its placement in the home with the death and inheritance of each successive family member.

Oddly enough, the first reports of ghostly activity at Strawbery Banke's Chase House started in the 1990s and has continued since then. If the ghost existed in this house before that time, it kept itself a secret for reasons known only to it. It is unusual, in a neighborhood dating back hundreds of years, to suddenly have a ghost pop up that was never there before. Ghosts and hauntings have been known to start up during times of renovations because ghosts tend to be very attached to their homes. They like things to stay the same as they were during their life. But Strawbery Banke's homes are kept as close to their original state as humanly possible and no major work was done on Chase Home at the same time as the haunting started to be publicized.

Though this room is closed off from visitors volunteers often find the bric-a-brac above the fireplace moved throughout the room, sometimes after they have closed for the night and they know they are alone in the building.

Stoodley's Tavern

Today, Stoodley's Tavern is the Lou and Lutza Smith Youth Learning Center at Strawbery Banke. It is used as an educational center for the student groups that frequent the museum. As an early meeting place for those who were to start the Revolutionary War, and as the place Paul Revere stopped to warn Portsmouth that British troops were about to seize the weapons at the local Fort, its value in New Hampshire and American history is incalculable. The building was moved to Strawbery Banke from a different section of Portsmouth in 1966 when it, and the houses on either side of it, went up for demolition.

But, of course, with such a long history, not all of it is as noble as that of freeing the burgeoning country from the rule of the Monarchy. In the 1760s, Stoodley's Tavern was also the scene of several auctions where slaves were placed on the auctioning block right next to barrels of rum or bales of cotton. It is said that in the basement of the site on Daniel Street from where the house was moved, there were two small cells where slaves were kept in squalid conditions until time came to auction them.

Today, Stoodley's Tavern is home to a prank-playing spirit that belies its Revolutionary and human trafficking history. Before the building was moved, neighbors on Daniel Street said they would sometimes see a gloved hand pull back the curtains and look out at them, even though they knew the building was long abandoned. The police were called out several times to chase away whoever it was living in the abandoned tavern, but when they investigated the building, they never found any evidence that anyone was living there.

This figure has not been visible since the house was disassembled and rebuilt at Strawbery Banke, but its presence is still sometimes felt. Cell phones are said to start ringing for no reason while in Stoodley's Tavern and the caller IDs come up as blank or long lines of nonsense numbers. Lights burn out at a faster-than-normal pace and sometimes click out all together. Several people have gotten odd photos with streaks of light blue lights or the orbs that parapsychologists tell us is evidence of the presence of ghosts.

Sherburne House

Sherburne House is the only seventeenth-century building at Strawbery Banke and it has a very overprotective ghost living there.

This ghost is often described as a gray lady, because of its drab gray gown and long melancholy face. Everyone who has encountered this ghost speaks of the sadness that emanates from it and its piercing protective glare. This ghost seems to be riled up by changes to the house; a new coat of paint or even the most minor of repairs cause a slew of sightings in the days that follow. It likes things quiet and kept the same.

The spirit is thought to belong to the daughter of the house's original builder, Captain John Sherburne. He died before the house was ever truly complete and the next owners not only bought the house, but took care of his mute daughter. As John Sherburne had eight daughters, and record keeping was not as organized or stringent as it is today, there is some debate about which of the eight Sherburne girls this was. Most likely it was Rebecca, though speaking that name at the house has no effect one way or another on its ghost.

The Sherburne House at Strawbery Banke Museum is watched over by a woman in gray who may date back to the late 1600's when the house was built.

The gray lady of Sherburne House is seen as much inside the small building as she is outside. Many visitors to Strawbery Banke have peered out of the unusual diamond-shaped panels of the windows of Sherburne House to see this ghostly figure floating around the garden out back. She is a slow-moving gray mist that flits between the raised vegetable beds, sometimes distinct enough to see that she holds a book in one wispy hand.

The Sherburne girl had a happy life at the house and those who have had a close encounter with her spirit feel no threat from her, as long as they treat her home with the respect she feels it deserves. She is not a frightening specter, simply a protective force watching over the changes to the house that she, and her father, loved so much in life.

Strawbery Banke Visitors Center

The Visitors Center itself doesn't seem to have ghostly residents inside. Outside is a different story. When work is being done on the Strawbery Banke buildings, and really there is just about always some type of work being done there, either to repair the buildings or for research purposes, a shrouded white figure hovers outside the Visitors Center. This indistinct white figure paces nervously, back and forth, back and forth, until the work settles down. When things are quiet at Strawbery Banke, the ghost is quiet. But as soon as work starts up again, so does the ghost.

Some people have questioned whether this spirit is the same as the gray lady at Sherburne House, since they both seem so protective of their homes. But the Sherburne ghost seems very much tied to that one house and oblivious of the changes in the neighborhood around it. Whoever this white figure is, it is a mystery. It could be a spirit of a former Strawbery Banke resident, one of the original creators of Strawbery Banke watching over their work, or even one of the many volunteers that have worked at Strawbery Banke over the years.

The William Pitt Tavern

The William Pitt Tavern has a colorful history. At the time it was built in 1750, taverns were not just places to go and relax for an evening over a glass of beer or for travelers to rest for a night. The William Pitt Tavern was the place you went to buy a newspaper and catch up on the news of the day. Taverns were a place to gather and discover your niche in your community. Business deals were made, friendships strengthened, and the community woven just a little more close knit. A plaque located outside the building says that George Washington himself visited the tavern.

The William Pitt Tavern was also the site of New Hampshire's first Mason lodge and it has some interesting architectural features because of this. One of the stairwells at the William Pitt Tavern was built to the far rear of the building so Masons could enter and exit the building without having to walk through the tavern itself. The Inn's fireplaces were placed at complete opposite ends of the building in order to leave a wide open space on the second floor to accommodate rooms for large gatherings in between.

The second floor also featured a "floating floor," thus named for the large amount of sand that was poured between the beams before the floorboards were placed on top. This completely soundproofed the room so the patrons of the tavern in the room below couldn't hear what went on above them. Just to be extra sure, grain chaff filled the space between the inner wall and outer walls so nothing said inside could be heard outside.

While the meetings held on the second floor were carefully-guarded secrets, what isn't so secret is how much most of the people who were in those meetings loved this meeting space—because many of their spirits still use the Pitt Tavern today! A psychic who visited the William Pitt Tavern, with no knowledge of its past, described in great detail the crowd of people in old-fashioned dress she saw walking around upstairs, laughing, and partying. Other people have seen shadows from the corners of their eyes while upstairs and a glowing mist that passes through the walls.

The Museum Shop at Dunaway Store

The Museum Shop looks old, blending in quite nicely with its well-preserved neighbors, but it was built as recently (in Strabery Banke time at least) as 1967. However, it was built directly on the site of a much older building that was too far past its prime to be saved. Most likely, the ghost that is seen in and around the Museum Shop actually belongs to that much older building.

The Museum Shop's ghost is a shy, quiet figure dressed as a minister and sometimes seen reading from his Bible. He is most often seen at dusk and has a mournful air about him. The ghostly minister is frequently seen walking around the building or inside peering from the windows as if he is waiting for something.

Beyond the Stars

Portsmouth's Long History of UFO Sightings and Alien Abductions

We tend to use the word paranormal or supernatural to refer to ghosts, poltergeists, and other spooks. But paranormal can refer to any extraordinary situation or event. While Portsmouth's history of alien abduction may not have anything to do with ghosts it is still unusual enough to be worth noting.

The Hill Incident

Today, UFO reports are so well reported, either by local media or tabloids, that they seem to be almost commonplace. Mainstream movies feature alien abductions fairly often. In1961, however, this was an entirely different story. UFOs and alien abductions were not taken seriously, widely reported, or mentioned outside of science fiction novels geared towards teenage boys.

A Portsmouth couple named Betty and Barney Hill were the first people to experience a widely reported alien abduction. The Hill Incident, as their experience came to be known, ushered in the modern era of alien abductions.

In September of 1961, the Hills were driving home to Portsmouth after a vacation. It was past the summer tourist season and leaf peepers, as New Hampshirians call the weekend road trippers who flock to the state to view the foliage, had not quite begun their fall migration. The roads were deserted. Suddenly, their attention was drawn to a bright point of light in the dark night sky. At first the Hills assumed they were seeing a falling star. Abruptly, the light shot upwards towards the moon.

The Hills still had no inkling that they were about to be confronted with something out of the ordinary. They were, in fact, sure that what they had just seen was a satellite. Unconcerned, they pulled over on the deserted road to walk their dog and stretch their legs after the long car ride. But as they walked the dog, the behavior of the strange light would attract their attention again. It buzzed around in front of and around the moon, flashing multi-colored lights. Betty began to question exactly what could be flying so erratically.

Back in the car, the lights continued to follow the Hills. As time went on, the lights got closer and closer, darting around and between mountains, speeding up and receding for no apparent reason. Without warning, the lights plummeted. They fell rapidly until directly in front of the Hill's 1957 Chevrolet, about 100 feet off the ground. Barney stopped the car in the middle of the isolated highway and grabbed a pair of binoculars from the backseat. He rushed outside to try and get a clear view of what had accosted them. Through the lens of the binoculars he saw eight to ten vaguely humanoid figures inside what he could now see was some kind of metallic ship.

Barney rushed back to the car, screaming at Betty that the creatures were there to capture them, even though he could not explain why he had that sudden intuition. The ship moved directly above the Chevrolet as the Hills sped off down the road. For the rest of the ride home they felt dull and dreamy, and were unable to tell if the ship was still above their vehicle or not. They were also plagued by strange metallic beeps and buzzes that seemed to have no source inside their car.

By dawn, they were home in Portsmouth but their troubles were far from over. Unpacking the car, Betty noticed her dress was torn and couldn't figure out how or why. She found a strange pinkish powder near the tears. Disgusted, she threw the garment outside, not wanting it in the closet near her other clothes but unable to throw it away for good. Left outside the powder soon disappeared, but it left pinkish stains that would go on to be the subject of countless scientific investigations when the story of her strange evening broke. She felt a strange need to leave a packed suitcase by the backdoor of the house and didn't know why.

When Betty and Barney sat down to talk about the encounter, they discovered that their memories were spotty. They both clearly remembered and described initially seeing the light and even the ship. But once they progressed to the part of the evening where the strange noises pursued their car, together they couldn't piece together a continuous chain of events. When Barney went out to unpack the car he discovered that, much like his wife's dress, the strap of his binoculars was also broken—yet one more thing from the night before he had no clear memory of happening.

Truly frightened, Betty called nearby Pease Air Force Base and reported what they had seen the night before. She was worried that she would be passed off as a lunatic so she didn't voice her fear that there may have been other things that happened that night that had been wiped from their memories. The Air Force was interested enough that they sent a Major out to talk with them. He told the Hills he was sure they had just misidentified the planet Jupiter, which was particularly bright that night, but he did forward a copy of his report to Project Blue Book.

Project Blue Book was a long-term study the U.S. Air Force conducted on unidentified plying objects. In the seventeen years Project Blue Book was active, they collected close to 13,000 different reports of strange lights, possible flying machines, and alien abductions. The vast, vast majority of these were deemed 'natural' phenomena, like Jupiter or fog, and many outright hoaxes were uncovered. There were over 700 separate incidences though that the Air Force admitted they could come up with no rational explanation for. Despite these 700 curious reports, the end result of the project was the official declaration that UFOs did not exist and were of no further concern to the United States government. Unofficially, there have long been rumors that the government continues to collect UFO data and that they have taken part in covering up evidence of alien visits to Earth.

The Hills were not put off by the Air Force discounting their encounter. Betty was having vivid nightmares every night of being escorted into a space craft and being examined by doctors inside. The dreams were so detailed and realistic, not to mention troubling, that she became convinced that they were not dreams at all but were rather memories of something she had actually experienced. Barney was not quite as sure as his wife, but he too began to dream or remember troubling things as well.

Betty began to read any reputable book or article she could find on aliens, though at the time, there was a severe lack of alien texts to be found in the non-fiction section of the local bookstore. Eventually she found one by a former Marine who was part of NICAP, a UFO research group that was not affiliated with the United States government. NICAP was extremely interested in the Hills' encounter, and with their help, the Hills were able to determine that there were three hours of missing time from their memories of that evening.

The Hills were open with friends, family, and their church about their possible abduction, but they never actively pursued attention over it. They were active within the very small community of alien research groups and, by chance, a reporter happened to hear about what happened to them. It was a full three years after their fateful fall encounter when the first newspaper article appeared about the Hills but the time lapse made no difference. It caused an instant sensation, setting off a chain of media attention that would end with a popular book, The Interrupted Journey, being written about the case. In a very short period of time, the Hills went from being quiet Portsmouth residents to being a national sensation.

Of course, not everyone was as convinced as Betty Hill was that their experience had been real. Even Barney Hill remained a little skeptical about the things he could not quite recall. Many people felt that the Hills had seen something strange and then convinced themselves that there was more to it than there really was. Some felt that the hypnotism NICAP subjected the Hills to may have muddled their already unreliable memories. The Hills were also unusual for their time because they were a mixed-race couple. It has even been speculated that they hallucinated the incident because of the mental pressure and stress of being an interracial couple in the early 1960s.

Betty Hill remained firm that what she had experienced was real up until her death in 2004. While experts debate the validity of her experience, to this day there is no doubt that the media attention brought to their case, nearly unheard of before that time, helped bring UFOs and alien abductions out of the shadowy world of B movies and into the mainstream consciousness.

A History of Visitations

The Hills may be the most famous people to have met up with aliens in New Hampshire, but they are not the only, and not the first. One of the earliest UFO reports (in modern times at least, the Native Americans of what became New Hampshire have many myths that people believe are evidence of much earlier encounters) also took place in Portsmouth.

In July of 1951, two military personnel stationed in Portsmouth made a report that they had seen a long flying object, a hundred feet or more in length, and five times as wide as it was long zipping around the area at unheard speeds. The men, who had quite a bit of flying experience themselves said the object was flying at speeds exceeding a thousand miles an hour and that it left a glowing trail behind it as it went. The object was only visible for about a minute but they were both able to describe it in detail. They said it was made of an unidentifiable gray metal that was speckled with black spots. No explanation was ever given for what they saw.

Modern Reports

Alien visitations to Portsmouth aren't just relegated to the past. UFOs have been seen consistently in the area and are still reported to this day. Rockingham County, in which Portsmouth is located, neither the largest or most populated country in the state, is however the one with the most UFO reports. It has three times as many reported alien encounters as Hillsborough, the second most UFO visited county.

In November of 1997, two people were driving to Maine when they saw a crescent-shaped craft in the sky directly in front of their car. When their vehicle approached the ship, it, much like in the Hill abduction, plummeted towards them. As it fell, its illumination increased until the occupants of the car were blinded. Just as abruptly, their vision cleared and the ship was gone. They exited the car and looked around trying to tell where it had disappeared to. But the ship was gone as if it had never existed.

This story, obviously reminiscent of the Hill abduction, is very typical of the UFO sightings around Portsmouth. The hundreds of UFOs that have been seen in and around Portsmouth all have the same very similar threads running through them.

An Unusual Intruder

A Ghost Breaks Into an Apartment Building in Portsmouth

I t was supposed to be a romantic evening for Jason and his girlfriend Heather. For once, all of Jason's roommates were gone for the weekend and they would have a chance to be alone. With three guys living in the small apartment, it was a rare occurrence to get to invite his girlfriend over.

The couple had just settled in on the couch to watch a movie when they heard the distinct rumble of the neighbors sliding-glass balcony door rumble. Jason glanced up at the sound, surprised. The next door neighbor was supposed to be away too, taking his kids on a camping trip. It had been all the neighbor would talk about for weeks. Being divorced, and living so far away from his ex wife, meant he didn't get to spend as much time with his kids as he would have liked to. Jason wondered vaguely what could have happened to cancel the trip.

With a sigh, he heaved himself up off the old couch and turned the television volume down. The guy next door didn't mind much about the noise, but Jason knew as well as anyone how thin the walls separating the apartments were. No sense not being a good neighbor. But when he turned the volume down a few notches, he was even more surprised to hear heavy footsteps pacing back and forth in the apartment next door. The neighbor definitely wasn't a big guy; Jason had never heard him make such a racket before just walking around his apartment. For that matter, the guy almost never used his balcony.

As he settled back onto the couch, wrapping his arms around Heather, he started to turn the situation over in his brain. Something just didn't feel right. Could there be an intruder in the next door apartment?

Jason cautioned himself to calm down. What was wrong with him? It wasn't like him to hear a few noises next door and jump to conclusions about burglars. He figured that his roommates being gone must be making him more cautious than normal. But just as he finally forced himself to relax, there was an enormous cacophony next door that sounded like someone was smashing glass and kicking the walls.

"What's happening?" Heather asked him, the movie forgotten.

Jason was already up off the couch and grabbing his phone. As he ran out his front door, he called back to Heather to lock their balcony door and keep watch in case the intruder left that way. From within the apartment they could hear what sounded like something heavy being dragged across the floor and more things crashing and breaking. Jason started to worry that something was about to come right through the walls into his own place!

Using his phone, Jason dialed the police and reported a robbery. The police arrived at the apartment building in just a few minutes. By the time they pulled up, the lady on the other side of the neighbor's apartment had come out to see what all the noise was about. When the police officer banged on the door and shouted for entry into the home, the noises stopped as suddenly as they had started. The people in the hallway paused for a minute, listening for more clatter. When there was no answer, the policeman knocked again. Still nothing.

The other neighbor produced a key for the apartment, as she had agreed to water the neighbor's plants while he was off camping with his kids. The cops took the key and warned everyone else to go back into their own apartments. When Jason walked in, Heather told him she had seen no movement through the curtained balcony door next door and that the intruder definitely hadn't left through that door.

The couple held their breath and listened to the cops quickly go through the small one-bedroom apartment next door. The sounds of their footsteps were much lighter than the ones they had just been listening to. Sometimes they heard the policemen call things out to each other, but they didn't sound terribly alarmed.

After a few minutes, it occurred to Jason that there was no intruder over there. If so, then surely they would have heard the police call out or chase the guy down. And he knew there was no way an intruder in the apartment could have gotten out without either Heather seeing them flee from the back balcony or seeing them come through the front door himself. There was no other exit or entrance to and from the apartment.

Jason's guess was correct. The police came out a few minutes later and talked to them again. They not only hadn't found any intruders, or any sign of forced entry, but they also hadn't found one thing in the apartment that looked out of place. Thankfully, the neighbor on the other side was there to back up Jason and Heather's claims of the breaking and dragging they'd heard!

A few days later, the owner of the apartment came back from his camping trip. He came over to thank Jason for watching out for his place while he was gone.

"I feel a little foolish," Jason told him. "The police sort of acted like it was a prank or something I was pulling."

"Well," the neighbor answered. "I'll tell you, I don't care what the police think one way or another. I walked in and every light bulb in the place is burned out. Every single one. And the apartment feels weird, like every time I walk in a room I expect someone to be there, but there never is."

The classic signs of a haunting continued after that. The neighbor complained to Jason about cold spots and phones that rang even when there was no one on the other line. His cell phone refused to work even though it showed he should have full service in the apartment. Sometimes it would ring, showing all zeros in the caller I.D. screen, and when he tried to answer the call, it wouldn't stop its incessant ringing. The neighbor didn't seem particularly worried about what might be going on and neither he nor Jason ever mentioned the word 'ghost.' But deep down, that is exactly what Jason thought the problem was.

Often, when Jason knew his neighbor was at work or away for the weekend, he would hear the unmistakable sounds of someone wandering around the next-door apartment. The woman on the other side mentioned it as well. The ghost didn't seem very scary, especially separated by a wall, but Jason always worried that if a ghost could move itself in to the apartment next door without warning, who was to say that another one wouldn't move itself into his own place?

The Haunted Islands of New Hampshire's Coast

There are nine islands making up the Isles of Shoals and they are split by New Hampshire and Maine. They are Smuttynose Island, Appledore, Star, Seavey, Malaga, Cedar, Lunging, Duck, and White. Despite their diminutive size, they have played a big role in the history and development of both of the states. They are located just ten short miles out to sea from Portsmouth and there is a ferry you can take from Portsmouth Harbor to visit some of the islands for the day.

Originally called Smith's Isles, in honor of Captain John Smith, the named was later changed to the Isle's of Shoals, for the abundance of shoals of fish which flourished near the islands, making them integral to the survival of first the Native Americans, and later the early European settlers. These settlers, or the Shoalers as they are affectionately known, have always had a reputation for being stubborn and more than a little odd. Some might consider them the truest of the true New Englanders! It is interesting to note that while every Shoaler knows the ghost tales surrounding their home and, if you can pry it out of them, most have experienced the ghosts themselves, it is the tourists who brought the stories back to the mainland. Even when looking at modern-day run-ins with ghosts or UFOs around the Isles of Shoals, it is always mainlanders who are doing the reporting. The Shoalers keep their tales to themselves.

Women were not allowed on the Isles of Shoals until a 1647 court ruling gave them the right. About thirty years later, the isles would see a large (well, large by Isles of Shoals standards, at any rate) influx of new blood when forty families packed up from the mainland and made Star Island their home in order to avoid taxation from the British. By the 1700s, the island chain's reputation took something of a nose dive when it became a haven for the most infamous pirates of the day. William Kidd, Edward 'Blackbeard' Treach, Sam 'Black' Bellamy, and a host of other infamous scoundrels all frequented the Isles of Shoals. We know at least on pirate buried treasure on one of the islands and rumor has had it for hundreds of years that there is even more treasure to be found.

The islands have always been a source of legend, folklore, and, of course, ghost stories. The famous poet Celia Thaxter grew up on Appledore Island and the best selling novel, Weight of Water, by Anita Shreve, is based on the real-life murders of two girls that took place on Smuttynose Island in 1873. The islands have a long literary history—famous author Nathanial Hawthorne visited the islands in the late 1800s . . . and even he commented on some of the ghostly stories surrounding the area. Unfortunately, many of the local legends of the islands are extremely close to those of the neighboring islands. With so many of the tales being hundreds of years old, there are great debates on just what exactly occurred on which island. Did Blackbeard leave a wife on Starr Island? Or was it Appledore where he left her? Or, perhaps, he left several different wives on several different islands. Different sources accredit many of these stories with different locations all within the island chain called the Isles of Shoals, which can make it hard for the modern-day folklorist to untangle where truth and fiction become one. Between this and the long standing recalcitrance of the Shoalers, it can be hard to track down proof in the historical record of even the most mundane tales—never mind the paranormal ones!

Sea Spirits

The Isles of Shoals have long been known to sailors as a maritime disaster waiting to happen. Or, to put a finer point on it, a disaster waiting to happen again and again. Captains unfamiliar with the area and sailors who have slacked off for the barest of moments have found themselves in sometimes fatal situations along the island chain. Because of this, there are several ghost ships that are known to roam the area around the islands.

The *Isidore*

The *Isidore* wrecked along the coast of the Isles of Shoals in 1842 and has been seen ever since, shrouded in mist, its sails in tatters. It can sometimes even be seen from the ocean shore in Portsmouth and it is said to foretell a terrible storm coming in from the sea. It is usually only seen for a few moments before disappearing into the fog.

Sea of Revenge

The second most seen ghost ship usually manifests itself in January around the anniversary of the date that it, and fourteen lives, were lost to the rocky shores of Smuttynose Island. Smuttynose at the time of the wreck was home to Sam Haley, the so-called King of the Isles of Shoals, of whom much legend and lore has been built around. Because of all the legends about Sam Haley, it is hard to know who exactly the man may have really been. We do know that Haley married an island girl, and that together, they had two sons and a whopping nine daughters! Sam Haley is said to have made it his habit to leave the lights burning in his house throughout the night to warn sailors that they were approaching the islands' rocky shore. When his oldest son, his namesake, stayed on Smuttynose Island as an adult, he followed in the tradition his father started.

But regardless of this precaution, in January of 1813, a Spanish ship crashed into the shoreline of Smuttynose and, over the next few days, fourteen bodies were found. Several bodies were found frozen to death, as though the sailors had tried to crawl up the long slope from the beach to the younger Sam Haley's house. Sadly, not even one of these sailors made it to the warmth and safety that the house would have provided. The young Sam Haley buried the bodies himself, marking the spots with rocks. But he didn't do it solely from the kindness of his heart. Records from the time show that he charged the town a burial fee for the work. In an interesting side note, modern-day archaeologists have examined the area, where the rocks still stay to this day, but they have found no evidence that bodies were ever buried there.

During the winter months, many people have seen the vague gray outlines of the sailors lined up along the shoreline, still waiting for rescue from the bitter New England winter. It is far more common for people report seeing their ship still sailing around the island rather than seeing the sailors themselves. The ship appears in distress, the decks overrun with frantic sailors trying desperately to keep it from going under.

This ship was long thought to be the Spanish frigate *Sagunto* but some modern evidence has raised the question of whether it may actually be the Concepcion from Caldiz. While we may not be sure which ship is there, there is little debate that its ghostly presence is seen routinely, sailing out of the fog, a ghostly beacon of a bygone era.

One can't help but wonder if the ship is still seen because of the violence and tragedy that surrounded it's crews demise or if the ghosts are somehow stuck on the island because they may have been denied a proper burial.

Historically, though, the most frightening ghost ship for sailors around the Shoals to catch a glimpse of was not an impressive shipwrecked gallon. It was instead a simple row boat manned by one small gray figure huddled against the choppy sea. For close to thirty years this unearthly row boat struck fear into the hearts of sailors from Italy and Portugal.

A woman, by some accounts the wife of one of the Isles of Shoals fisherman, was stabbed to death on a boat manned by Portuguese and Italian fishermen. When her husband received the news of her death, he fled the Isles in a rickety old row boat during a terrible storm. The smashed remains of the boat were found the next morning and the fisherman presumed lost at sea. It was a great tragedy for the small close-knit community of the Isles of Shoals.

However, for the next thirty years, Italian and Portuguese sailors were attacked in the dead of night when they got too close to the Isles. No witnesses to the mutilations were ever found alive though more than a few of the dead men's crew members said they saw an old row boat driven by a single occupant in the vicinity of their ship the same night as the murders. No living person was ever charged with the crimes and the superstitious seamen stopped fishing near the Shoals for many decades.

It has been many, many years since any similar crimes have been reported near the islands but people claim, to this day, to see the gray rowboat sailing aimlessly around the waters of the Isles of Shoals on quiet foggy nights looking to avenge a murder that occurred centuries before.

Blackbeard and his Unlucky Wives

Edward Treach began life sometime in the late 1600s in a quiet shipping village on the English coast. By the 1700s, he would come to be called Blackbeard, and the notorious pirate is known by the hirsute moniker to the present day. There is a great deal of myth that has been built up about the pirate, and much of it was purposely cultivated by the great pirate himself. Blackbeard kept the Caribbean in terror for just a few short years, in what is usually called the "golden age of piracy," but he remains probably the most famous pirate to ever have lived, even today.

Blackbeard never allowed himself to be seen without his enormous feathered tricorn hat and, armed for any eventuality, he always wore a vast array of swords, knives, and pistols. He braided hemp yarn and matches into his beard that he would light on fire during battles, fighting with a dark cloud of smoke billowing around his terrifying face. Many people didn't bother to fight, and simply surrendered, rather then come face to face with this fearsome apparition who attacked them surrounded by stinking billowing dark clouds of smoke. During Blackbeard's lifetime, there were those who claimed he was Satan himself.

Even in life, the tales of his exploits grew to wild proportions, and time has only added to the incredulity of some of them. Blackbeard has been accused of everything from periodically killing his crew, to keep future crews in line, to watching as the crew took intimate liberties with whoever his current wife was at the time. The truth is that Blackbeard was one of the most humane and employee-friendly pirates to have ever sailed the seven seas. It is actually believed that Blackbeard never killed anyone and relied solely on his reputation to put fear into the hearts of his crew and captives. Blackbeard is known to have run a tight ship, to have followed pirate laws to the letter, and even offered a type of disability and life insurance to the men who sailed with him. A pirate that was injured fighting alongside Blackbeard was taken care of for the rest of his life and if he died, a settlement would reach his family.

But, of course, Blackbeard is not known for these kindnesses or even his mastery of propaganda. In the end, there are two things that Blackbeard has remained most known for, the first of which is his many wives. Although true facts are sketchy at best, and as a pirate Blackbeard didn't bother with such niceties as reported church weddings, the pirate is said to have married, and killed, as many as fourteen wives. The only story that overshadows his overzealous matrimonial leanings is the one about his treasure. It has long been rumored that Blackbeard had acquired a vast and unmatched treasure during his pirate days and that he buried this treasure . . . well, somewhere. You'll find rumors of Blackbeard's treasure being buried everywhere from Jamaica, to the Carolinas, to, of course, the Isles of Shoals. No matter how often historians point out the unlikelihood that Blackbeard's stolen booty ever amounted to anything more then the $2,500 he got when he sold his ship upon retirement, and that there is even less evidence that Blackbeard ever buried any of his earnings, the stories have gained too much strength over the years to be so easily forgotten.

Many of the treasure stories have gained a foothold in the tiny Isles of Shoals, and there are more then a few ghost stories that surround the rumors as well. The historian Richard Cahill believes that Blackbeard's treasure is buried on Lunging Island, and the stories that the ghost of the pirate himself seems to add weight to this theory. Many people who have seen the ghost say that it looks as though the apparition is searching for something, as if the location of the treasure may be lost even to him. Others hold fast to the idea that Blackbeard's ghost knows exactly where he left his gold and is there to protect it from being discovered. The spirit of Blackbeard is said to appear, surrounded by thick black haze, and dressed in 1700s pirate finery. Even in death, he refuses to be seen without his plumed triangular hat!

Lunging Island is also the site of one of the Isles of Shoals famous "Lady Ghosts." Like many of the chains' Lady Ghosts, she is thought to be one of Blackbeard's wives, who was abandoned on the island by the pirate when he saw the sails of an enemy ship approaching. Treach implored his wife to stay on the island and warn off anyone who came looking for the treasure, making her vow she'd remain faithful to him, and his treasure, until Doomsday if need be. Foolishly, the young girl agreed and nothing is known of her life or how she eventually died. However, much is known of her afterlife. She is sometimes seen crying, walking the beach agitatedly in a long sea cloak, with a jumble of sea-blown blond hair. She stands on the rocks overlooking the sea expectantly, and can be heard softly whispering, "He will return." If the ghost of Blackbeard is on Lunging Island, it would seem he's made a point of not reintroducing himself to his forlorn young wife.

There have also been reports of the ghost of Blackbeard's wives on both Smuttynose and White Island. But no one is sure if they are all the same ghost, searching for her wayward husband, or if they are the ghosts of several different wives. If Blackbeard had luck 'divorcing' one wife with an island abandonment, who is to say he didn't use the same trick on a few of his other unlucky wives, as well?

Appledore Island

Blackbeard was not the only pirate to venture to the Isles of Shoals, and he is not the only ghostly pirate that still walks them. A fearsome male specter on Appledore Island, most often described as having glowing red eyes, is said to be that of Phillip Babb. Babb was once the constable of Appledore Island, but before that he was a crewmate of the infamous pirate Captain Kidd. Babb's ghost is sometimes joined by a second apparition, also a former crew member of Captain Kidd, who was killed by the pirate Captain when they stopped ashore to bury treasure there. It is unclear if these two sailors are guarding the treasure, long rumored but never discovered, or if they themselves, even after death, are looking for it.

Ocean Born Mary

It is interesting that Babb's ghost is still such a prominent resident of the Isles as he is linked, factually or tenuously depending on who you hear the story from, with one of New Hampshire's most firmly entrenched, if slightly ridiculous, local legends that ends in persistent tales of haunting.

Ocean Born Mary is an old New England favorite that is as controversial as it is beloved. Like most legends, it certainly has a good deal of basis in fact. In 1720, the Foultans were Irish immigrants sailing to New England to start a new life for themselves. Considering that Elizabeth Foultan gave birth during the boat ride over, they certainly had a lot of motivation—and a great deal of bad luck. Some where around the Isles of Shoals, their ship was overtaken by pirates who quickly divested the passengers of whatever meager possessions they had.

The pirates, whom many sources say were led by Phillip Babb, were debating whether or not to kill the shipload of people, the Foultans' newborn babe began to wail, revealing the place where her parents had hidden her. Undoubtedly, the passengers were alarmed when the pirates pulled the child from its hiding spot but, inexplicably, the pirate captain said he would free everyone on board so long as the parents of the baby would agree to name her Mary, after the Captain's mother. The Foultans, of course, quickly agreed.

At this point, story tellers begin a decidedly sharp veer away from fact into romanticism. Supposedly, the pirate crew not only spared everyone's life but they also bestowed upon the newborn baby a thick bolt of green silk cloth that was meant to someday be the girl's wedding gown. The historical society in Concord has a few small scraps of cloth that are said to be from this fabled bolt, but this part of the story seems to be unlikely, at best.

We know from records that Mary and her family did make it to New Hampshire and that they moved from town to town for awhile. Mary was wed in 1742, supposedly in her green brocaded pirates silk and went on to have four or five children. After being widowed, Mary would move to Henniker to stay with one of her sons and live in obscurity until her death at the ripe old age of 94.

Legend, of course, is not quite as willing to assign Mary such a humble life. Some versions of the legend say that the pirate came back for Mary and married her himself. Others say that the pirate tracked her down and built a fine house where Mary worked as a housekeeper. Mary has been seen, in various legends, as stealing away with pirates treasure and burying it, inheriting pirate's treasure, or sailing away on a pirate's schooner.

In Henniker, New Hampshire, you can find the "Ocean Born Mary House," where Mary has been proven time and time again to have never lived, but where her ghost is said to walk perpetually, either looking for her buried treasure or making sure to keep it safe from would-be treasure hunters. Her pirate lover, possibly Babb though it would be quite a trip to go from Appledore Island to Henniker so routinely, has also been seen.

It may be worth mentioning though that for all the fanciful tales surrounding Ocean Born Mary, she did at least live on the same street as the house that has been named after her and ghostly activity has been reported at many of the other properties there. Female ghosts seem to be most prevalent, though no one has mentioned if they are wearing gowns of green silk.

The Lady Ghost

Appledore Island also has a Lady Ghost of its own. The Lady Ghost of Appledore may be another one of Blackbeard's wives, or his unlucky wife traveling from Lunging Island to Appledore searching for her wayward husband. Other people believe she is Martha Gordon who was the common-law wife of Andy "the Scott," a pirate who was a close friend and colleague of Blackbeard's.

Martha Gordon was left behind on Appledore Island by Andy the Scott when his men mutinied at the thought of setting sail with a woman on board. Sailors have long been known for their superstitions and one of the oldest pieces of seafaring wisdom was that women had no place at sea. It was thought that if a woman were aboard a ship, it was doomed to sink. Either the men would fight amongst themselves over the woman or a great storm would come and smash the ship to smithereens. This belief was doubly ironic considering how common it was, even at that time, for the figurehead of the ship to be a nude woman or mermaid. Women were thought to be better navigators with clearer sight, so the female figurehead was a symbolic way of keeping the ship on course—even if a real woman was not allowed on board.

Like Blackbeard was said to do to his wives, Martha Gordon was left behind, waiting for a husband who never returned for her, or for any treasure he was rumored to have left behind.

The Demonic Butcher

The most frightening ghost of the Isles of Shoals can be found on Appledore Island. This frightening specter dates back to when an argumentative and greedy butcher lived on the island. Legend says that one day he discovered a large chest tucked into a smoking stinking hole formed by a fissure in a large piece of granite bedrock. Convinced he had found a pirates stash, the butcher worked trying to dislodge the heavy chest. After working for some time, day and night without rest. he was overcome by the heat and sulfur pouring through the hole. He was found by his neighbors raving about pirate's gold, but no one ever found the treasure chest in the hole filled with smoke. Within a few days, the butcher died of exhaustion.

It was not long after his death that reports sprang up of people seeing the butcher slinking around the island at night. Early stories described him as looking gray and shambling awkwardly but looking, for the most part, more or less, alive. As time went on, the butcher became more frightening looking. He is now said to appear as a rotting corpse dressed only in the tattered remnants of his clothes and a blood-splattered butcher's apron. Even more alarmingly, this grim figure has been seen holding a knife in his hand.

Many people at the time said that the man had made an ill-fated deal with the Devil, exchanging his soul for a chest full of gold, and that the Devil had gotten the best of him, as the Devil usually does in these cases. Others said that because the man had died of his avarice, he was not allowed through Heavens Gate's and that the man decided to stay on Earth to avoid going to Hell. Still others felt that the butcher stayed on simply to continue working away at trying to recover the mysterious chest full of pirate gold. This story is supported by the ghostly shovels that are sometimes found on the island, the ones that disappear when living people walk up to them to investigate. Celia Thaxter, the poet of the Isles, may have summed it up best when she said that the butcher was so desperately wicked when he was alive that there was no rest for him in his grave.

White Island

Besides Blackbeard's wives, there are several other ghosts occupying White Island, both of them terribly tragic. Around Moody's Cave on the island a horrifying shrieking specter is heard and even sometimes seen. She is what remains of Betty Moody. Nathanial Hawthorne wrote about hearing the unearthly noises during his visits to the Isles of Shoals. When asking his host what could make such a desolate horrifying sound, he was told that the noises came from the spirit of Betty Moody, who had lived on the island long ago. One night, some of the Native American population came from the mainland to the island, presumably to plunder it. Betty Moody heard the cry of murder come up from some neighboring houses and gathered her child, or children to her, and fled to the caves to hide. The child, or children as the records are unclear, were frightened to be woken up at midnight, and even more scared to be brought to this long low cave were they huddled with their frantic mother. They began to cry and Betty, fearful the noise would cause them to be discovered, murdered them in order to save herself. Wracked by guilt at what she had done in life, her spirit now forever roams outside the cave where she committed such a heinous act.

The other White Island ghost dates back to the mid 1800s when a local school teacher used to spend her lunch time sitting on the rocks overlooking the ocean. On day before a storm disaster struck, the teacher was knocked down, and knocked out, by one wave that crashed upon the rocks where she was sitting. Then a second wave dragged her body out to sea where no one could rescue her. The teacher's body was never found. Her ghost, however, can still be seen on the very same rocks overlooking the ocean. She appears before storms to warn the living away from the spot where she lost her life all those years ago.

Smuttynose Island

In 1873, three young Norwegian women were set upon by a killer on Smuttynose Island. Karen Anne Christensen and Anethe Matea were strangled to death, and one of them was struck with a hatchet. A third woman, Maren Hontvet, managed to escape and hid herself in a small cave among the rocks on the shore. She would survive to identify the man who killed her friends, the man who almost killed her. She said that a German fisherman, Louis Wagner, was the killer and he was quickly sentenced to hang. Maren had no doubt that the killer was Wagner but he passionately maintained his innocence to his execution and was so convincing that, to this day, people still debate if he was actually guilty. The story would go on to become the basis for Anita Shreve's bestselling novel, The Weight of Water, which went on to be adapted to the big screen as a movie starring Sean Penn and Elizabeth Hurley.

A few years after the murders, the house where the site of the grisly double murders occurred burnt to the ground. All in all, the inhabitants of Smuttynose Island were happy to see the reminder of the unhappy time go. But the trouble wasn't over by a long shot. Soon after the house disappeared into flames, people reported seeing a ghostly figure that looked strikingly like Louis Wagner wandering around the area. Some people claim that the spirit is a remorseful one, tied forever to the place where he did such a terrible act; other people say that Wagner was innocent of the crimes and that his spirit haunts, and will haunt, the area until his innocence has been proven. Interestingly, the victims of the crime are also famous ghosts; they however haunt Portsmouth's South Cemetery, where they are buried.

Star Island

No less then three floors of Star Islands' popular Oceanic Hotel are haunted. The first floor men's room is the unlikely home of one of these ghosts, who is something of a spectral Peeping Tom. Patrons of this bathroom report feeling as though someone is watching them when there is no one visible in the room with them and to hearing an incessant knocking while they use the restroom, even when other people assure them there is no one there. There are at least two different ghosts who haunt the third and fourth floors of the hotel, slamming doors, pushing around furniture, and digging through bureau drawers as though they are searching for something. The fourth floor of the hotel is used as an attic, completely devoid of furniture and heavy objects, but you would never be able to guess at its emptiness when standing on the third floor. Once the attic ghost gets going, you hear the sound of heavy footsteps and even heavier furniture being shoved from one side of the building to the other. Go up and investigate and you'll find nothing that could produce such noise.

The Beebe Family Cemetery

On the grounds of the Oceanic Hotel you can find the ancient Beebe Family Cemetery. Long before the Oceanic Hotel existed, back in 1857, Reverend George Beebe came to Star Island to act as a missionary to the island. There were less then 100 people living here at this time and, as the island was a popular retreat for tuberculosis patients, that number was dwindling all the time. Partially out of charity, partially to fill time, Reverend Beebe started the first cemetery on Star Island, clearing the land with his own hands. He never could have imagined that the only graves to ever grace this cemetery would be that of his own daughters.

In 1863, Reverend Beebe's entire family fell ill with consumption, as TB was called at the time. Three of his daughters died and were buried in the cemetery their father had created. Their pious gravestones stand there to this day. Millie Beebe's reads, "Dying she kneeled down and prayed: Jesus, take me up to the lighted place. And he did." The marker of her older sister, Mitty, only seven when she died, says simply, "I don't want to die, but I'll do just as Jesus wants me to." The third tombstone is, after well over 100 years near the sea, unreadable. We know from historic records that this third Beebe sister was named Jessie, and was aged two at death, but know nothing of what the inscription of her grave may have said.

In modern times, visitors to Star Island did not even realize there was a cemetery there. The white iron railing and arched gate, that surrounded the spot had been removed years before and the undergrowth completely covered all signs of the graves. Even so, the Beebe girls were not ready to be forgotten so easily. People often saw flashes of a young child running through the trees, or would catch a young woman's voice reciting Bible verse when there was no speaker present. The laughter of children sometimes carried hauntingly on the ocean breeze, or the sounds of a young girl comforting a crying baby. The ghosts were a mystery until the family plot was discovered.

The Beebe Family cemetery has since been cleared of the obscuring trees and weeds and because the upkeep on the land has continued, all signs of ghostly activity have disappeared.

Vampires of the Shoals

The Beebe sisters may, or may not, be the spirits who roam the island and scratch at windows at night as though they are trying desperately to get inside. Less commonly, people hear soft indecipherable whispering to accompany the scratching. Some people have passed the noise off as a freak weather occurrence, the ocean wind whistling through tree branches, creating both the whispering and the scratching. Others, once the Beebe Cemetery was found, chalked it up to the young sisters trying to warn visitors away from the island. But there is some evidence that the noise was reported by visitors long before the Beebe family ever set foot on Star Island. Chillingly, many early accounts of the phenomena put the blame squarely on the shoulders of vampires. While today we think of vampires as belonging to dark Transylvanian castles, the belief in these bloodthirsty creatures of the night was quite widespread in the early part of the history of the United States, and deeply rooted in the folk beliefs of New England.Interestingly, tuberculosis was often misdiagnosed as 'proof' of vampire visitation so it should, perhaps, not come as a surprise that an island popular as a tuberculosis retreat was also thought to be a haunting ground for vampires.

Lakawaka

Lakawaka is, possibly, not a ghost at all but something much more fearsome. Could the Isles of Shoals be not just haunted but plagued by a sea monster as well? There are several mentions of this "Lakawaka" dating as far back as the early 1800s. It appears just off the shore of the islands (almost all nine have reports of Lakawaka) as a glowing worm of unimaginable proportions. Lakawaka is thought to be a female creature and is often seen watching over the body of her dead mate.

There is a Scottish tradition of family and friends watching over the body of the recently deceased to make sure it cannot be inhabited by demons before it is properly buried. The Scottish called this process "lyke-wake," and it is where the glowing worm creature of the Shoals got its name.

The sightings of Lakawaka were rare even in the 1800s and the accounts varied from a mysterious sea creature to that of a more ordinary ghost. There have been no modern-day reports of the creature. Perhaps her husband was finally laid to rest and the lyke-wake ended?

Boon Island Lighthouse

Boon Island is not considered to be part of the Isles of Shoals today, but for much of history it was included in the island chain and it is still visited by the Isles of Shoals Steamship Company which gives tours of the islands. It certainly has enough ghosts to count it in with the rest of the islands! Boon Island is composed of roughly 400 yards of barren rock. The famous Isles of Shoals poet, Celia Thaxter, described it as, "The forelornest place that can ever be imagined."

Boon Island got its name in 1682 when four men washed up on its desolate shores after their ship, the Increase, wrecked on the rocks. The four survivors managed to last a month living on the island with no shelter and eating only fish and gulls eggs. After seeing a fire burning on the mainland, they built their own signal fire in response and the local Native American tribe came and rescued them. The survivors saw their rescue as a gift from God and named the pile of rocks "Boon Island." The name stuck despite the fact that for many years only tragedy would fall upon all those who were unlucky enough to find themselves on Boon Island.

The next shipwreck survivors to end up on Boon Island were not nearly so lucky. In 1710, Nottingham Galley, a British ship, wrecked near the island. For nearly a month the crew of Nottingham Galley faced harsh conditions and finally resorted to cannibalism in order to live. Once they were discovered, emaciated, near mad, and half dead, local fisherman from the Isles of Shoals started to leave casks of food and water on Boon Island in case anyone else washed up on its unforgiving shores in the future.

Nearly eighty years later, the first of a succession of beacons and lighthouses was built on Boon Island in the hopes of warding off wrecks and to help fisherman keep their bearings. During the construction of the second lighthouse, after the first collapsed during a storm, two construction workers drowned when their boat capsized as they left the island.

The ill luck continued on Boon Island with the arrival of lighthouse keepers who manned the beacon. After one fierce week-long storm, local fishermen noticed that the light was out in the stone tower and sailed to Boon to investigate. They found the lighthouse keeper's young wife wandering around the rocks, as the ocean crashed forward to sweep her away, driven insane by lack of sleep and crushing grief. Her husband had died in his sleep while they were cut off from the outside world during the storm and the young woman heroically took on his duties herself for the duration of the week. Every time the light went out, she would trudge up the tower's 170 stairs and relight it herself. As the storm raged on, she became increasingly paranoid that the light had gone out and would race up the stairs to check on it. While she undoubtedly saved many lives that week, the cost to the young bride was her sanity. The young woman died a few weeks later and was buried next to her husband.

The ghost most often seen on Boon Island may be that of the young bride, though some stories claim she was the mistress of the captain of the Nottingham Galley. The spirit appears dressed in white, with a long sad face, wandering aimlessly from place to place. In the 1970s, the crew manning the Boon Island lighthouse went out fishing and were delayed returning in time to light the tower. However, when they made it back to Boon, the lighthouse was glowing brightly. There was not one other person left on the island that day so they were forced to conclude that the spirit must have gone up the stairs to light the tower one last time.

Other people who have lived at Boon, Lighthouse keepers, their families, even members of the Coast Guard, have had experiences with ghosts on Boon. Doors open and shut without cause, the sound of footfalls is heard often. A Labrador Retriever that stayed on the island was known for chasing nothing that his human masters could see from one side of the island to another.

Seacoast Spirits

Portsmouth isn't the only haunted town on New Hampshire's seacoast. Just a short drive from the city's downtown area offers a wealth of ghostly attractions. During one day trip in and around the city of Portsmouth you can find, literally, dozens of haunted locales to explore.

Dover

Slightly larger in population than Portsmouth, Dover is the oldest permanent settlement in New Hampshire, and is the seventh oldest in the United States. The most commonly seen ghost in Dover dates back to some of the darkest events in the town's history.

Salt Eye Storr

Richard and William Storr were brothers who often didn't see eye to eye. William was the church-going Puritan, while Richard, the younger of the two, ran away to a life at sea at the age of twelve. Richard made sea captain by the time he was twenty and was known for his eccentric ways, but fair and generous treatment of his crew. After many years at sea, he decided to retire and moved to Dover to be near his only remaining relative. Richard, known by the nickname "Salt-Eye," built a small log cabin at the edge of town and settled into a contentious enough life there that his brother started spelling his last name differently so no one would realize they were related. But Dover was growing, and quickly, what was the edge of town when Salt Eye took up residence, wasn't on the outskirts for long. The town was springing right up alongside Salt Eye's doors, which meant that it was also quickly encroaching on the land of the local Native American tribe. The town wanted to grow but both Salt Eye and the Natives were refusing to budge.

In an amazing act of cowardice, Major Waldron invited the Native Americans to take place in a mock battle against his militia for the entertainment of some visiting British officials. But the mock battle was all a sham. When 400 members of the local Abenaki tribe showed up, Waldron placed them in chains and sent them off to Boston where some were executed and the rest sold off to slavery. Salt Eye Storr decried the villainy that took place right outside his front door, but few people paid heed. Now there was room for the city to expand unhindered and the British were so pleased with Major Waldron he was named Chief Justice for New Hampshire. In protest, Storr took to wearing traditional Abenaki garb himself and kept to himself in his cabin in the woods.

Thirteen years passed by without incident and the "mock war" that had meant such heartache for the local Abenaki tribe was forgotten by the citizens of Dover.

But the Abenaki didn't forget so easily. Thirteen long years later, they snuck into the city, burned several homes and mill houses, capturing or killing more then a quarter of the population. Major Waldron died at the hands of the Abenaki. The major's own sword was taken from him and used to make the killing blow.

Salt Eye Storr was left untouched in his cabin at the edge of town and wasn't aware of the massacre until the next day when he went into town to pick up supplies. As a sea captain, he had some rudimentary knowledge of medicine so he walked from home to home, helping all the survivors he could find. When he was done tending to the townspeople, he walked home to his cabin and returned to a solitary existence until the end of his days.

But even in death, Salt Eye Storr watches over the residents of Dover. He appears as a great glowing orb, about a foot in diameter, floating several feet off of the ground wandering the streets of old Dover. He most often appears on foggy nights and around the June anniversary of the massacre. Most of the sightings take place at the intersection of Central Avenue and Washington Street, though he has been seen near the post office and by the waters edge.

Cocheo Mills

In downtown Dover you can still find some of the old mills that once made this an important manufacturing city. These mills fell out of fashion, into disrepair, and are currently back in style once more. They are no longer used as manufacturing plants, but have been converted into everything from high-priced condominiums to office space. The Cocheo Mills in Dover are some of the latter.

The mills, however, don't forget their past lives so easily. Mill work in the early part of America's Industrial Revolution was hard, long, dirty work. Accidents were common; so were fatalities. In the long hallways of the Cocheo Mills, janitors have complained of hearing ghostly voices, yelling out orders to each other and, sometimes, screaming for help. Sometimes the voices are so loud that even people walking outside have heard them.

From outside the building, at night, people also see strange lights hovering around the upper floors of the mill and even in the long sealed-off basement. Perhaps most eerily, the mill seems to be haunted by the machinery that once filled its length. Vibrations and the grinding chugging noises of machines that are no longer there are as common as the ghostly voices of the men, women, and even children that once ran them.

The Ghost Train

The residents of the apartment building located on Folsom Street are kept up all night by the noise of the train that passes by the building. What's worse is that train has been out of service for more than sixty years!

Despite the fact that the train tracks have been blacktopped over, and the train line closed longer ago than most of the Folsom Street tenants have been alive, more nights than not, residents hear the train and its vibrations shake the building down to its very foundations.

Durham

The Three Chimneys Inn

The Three Chimneys Inn is thought to be one of the oldest surviving homes in the state. It was built in 1649 as the private residence of Valentine Hill. It is Hill's daughter, Hannah, that haunts the building today.

The beautifully renovated building is a first-class inn and the staff of this inn has a certain affection for their ghost. Hannah seems to enjoy having them around as well. Employees have had unique job perks such as having the ghostly Hannah play with their hair, or suddenly come face to face with her in the early hours of the morning. Hannah seems to have a penchant for pulling cabinet and desk drawers open, but her true love is anything electrical.

Calculators display numbers backwards, computer systems refuse to work, printers and faxes spit out papers long after their print jobs are finished—and even after having their plugs pulled! Hannah despises change in the building so workers can always count on her interfering with anything electrical that she thinks is going to be used to change the home she loves.

Hannah, the daughter of the builder of the Three Chimney's Inn, continues eternally as hostess at the charming bed and breakfast.

Several people have seen items in the Inn levitate and a few have even seen a visible manifestation of the spirit known as Hannah. Due to the sheer age of the building, and the massive amount of ghostly activity reported there, many people believe that Hannah is the most outgoing of the Three Chimneys Inns ghosts. There may be as many six restless spirits roaming the hallways of this lovely inn.

A male spirit has been seen quite often, particularly inn the room called the "Coppers Dining Room." This spirit may be Valentine Hill himself or possibly Hannah's husband. Enough records survive for us to know that Hannah was married, somewhere around the age of twenty, and it is believed that she drowned in a nearby river.

Hampton

Just fourteen miles south of Portsmouth is the town of Hampton. It is best known as a popular summer tourist destination spot since it is home to Hampton Beach. It is also the locale of several rather famous tales from American folklore that are based on actual Hampton residents, Jonathan Moultan and Eunice "Goody" Cole.

The Witch of Hampton

Goody Cole, born in England in the late 1500s, is famous for being the only woman to be convicted of witchcraft in the state of New Hampshire. Goody Cole moved to New England with her husband in 1637, and the pair moved from town to town up the seacoast until they settled in Hampton about a year later. Goody Cole was known for her fierce temper and disagreeable ways. She was fervent believer of antinomianism, the idea that Christians were under no religious, civic, or moral obligation to follow the laws of any Government or religious authorities. The belief, added to her overall ill-natured personality, did nothing to endear her to her neighbors. Joseph Dow, author of History of the Town of Hampton, NH, has said of Eunice Cole " . . . she was both hated and feared" and "She was said to be, ill-natured and ugly, artful and aggravating, malicious and revengeful." Certainly not the description of a nice person to have living in your neighborhood.

Eunice would go to court several times between 1645 and 1656, charged with making slanderous speeches, before finally being charged as a witch in 1656. The court maintained that she was in league with the Devil, and there had long been grumbling from the townsfolk over a well on her property that never went dry or turned brackish. Because she lived close to a well-traveled river, many travelers made it a point to stop at her well for a sweet cool drink of water before they went on their way. As you can imagine, with her dislike of people, the practice drove Goody Cole mad. She would stand out on her back stairs and scream at people who used her well for water and, from time to time when an accident later occurred to the ones she'd been yelling at, people started to say the curses were real.

At the trial, another neighbor stood up and testified that Eunice warned him to keep his calves off her property or they'd choke on every blade of her grass they ate. Soon after, one of the calves died, and another disappeared completely. Add in some wild stories about devil dwarves from the young town's children and the case against Goody Cole was signed and sealed. In the end, the courts were, for their time period, lenient on the old woman. She was sentenced to a whipping and life in jail. Believe it or not, she got off easy; technically, she could have been executed for her crimes. She ended up being released and convicted several more times before her death.

Eunice Cole was dogged for the rest of her days by Hampton residents, who were more then a little unhappy to have her come back to live out the rest of her days in a shack at the foot of Rand's Hill near where the Tuck Museum stands today. When she died, the story goes, her body was dragged from the filthy shack where she spent her golden years and buried in a nearby ditch. Before interring the body, her neighbors drove a stake through her heart and hung an iron horseshoe atop it to keep the devil away. The grave was left unmarked, far from any cemeteries, and to this day has not been found. There are two "gravestone" memorials to Goody Cole in Hampton, but neither marks where her body is actually buried.

In 1939, with Eunice Cole dead in an unmarked grave for hundreds of years long passed, the residents of Hampton voted in favor of exonerating her of her charges. The official court documents condemning her as witch were burned on Hampton Beach and, mixed with soil from the area where her home stood, then were placed in an urn that can still be seen today at the Tuck Museum.

But even being declared innocent of any crime is not enough for Eunice Cole. The witch's ghost can still be seen in and around Founder's Park. Some people say they have felt her long bony fingers pinching them and slapping at them when they walked across the grass. This has led to some speculation that her body may have been

This stone, located at the Tuck Museum, is one of the modern day memorials to Goody Cole. The memorial stones on either side of it are marked with plaques but the Historical Society keeps this one unmarked to discourage Halloween vandalism.

buried in the vicinity of the park. She has also been seen, and felt, in the main building of the Tuck Museum.

Several people have been approached by a wild haired woman, in ragged old-fashioned clothing, in the oldest parts of town. Some have even spoken with the woman who they say asks continually about the whereabouts of some of Hampton's oldest families. In the 1950s a housewife saw this apparition, never realizing it was a ghost, and invited the woman inside for some lemonade. The little old woman started yelling about not being able to find the Goody Cole memorial on the village green and the housewife told her that it hadn't been erected yet. At this point, the old woman thanked her for the lemonade and walked out of the house—straight through the closed front door!

Jonathon Moultan Makes a Deal with the Devil

Jonathon Moultan would have had some sympathy for poor old beleaguered Eunice Cole. He wasn't much liked by his Hampton neighbors either, although for very different reasons. Moultan was a true success story, a self-made man who was known first as a Revolutionary War hero, then later as the wealthiest man in town. Only, some Hampton residents thought it was all a little too good to be true and decided that the only way Moultan could be as rich as he was,

The Tuck Museum is found in the back part of the building that is home to the Historical Society.

was if he had sold his soul to the Devil in exchange for it.

So the story began that once a month Jon would put his boots by the fire and the Devil would come while everyone slept and fill them with gold. But as time went on, two boots full of gold coins weren't enough for the greedy Jon Moultan. First he had a local cobbler make him the largest boots he could, ones easily twice the size as a normal mans foot would fit. When they were completed, Moultan placed the giant boots next to the fireplace as though they were his own and then went upstairs to what must have been a fitful slumber. Would the Devil be tricked by his ruse? It would seem he was, for the next morning there they stood, filled to the top with glittering gold coins.

Moultan was overjoyed, but as you can probably guess, after a few months went by, even this double amount wasn't nearly enough gold for him. Finally, he hit upon a clever idea. That night he cut the bottoms off the boots, placed them next to the fireplace, and then drilled holes through where the soles of the shoes should have been and clear into the basement underneath. When the Devil came to fulfill his end of the bargain, no matter how much gold he poured into the boots he couldn't get them full, because of course, unbeknownst to him they were pouring directly into the cavernous basement beneath Moultan's house. The Devil kept pouring, and the basement kept getting fuller and fuller, and finally, in a pique of anger, the Devil burned Moultan's house down.

Not repentant in the slightest, Moultan rebuilt the house in the same spot in 1769. It still stands today. Always in the mind to save some pennies, and apparently not superstitious in the slightest, Moultan even reused some of the Devil scorched bricks from the fireplace of his old home to build the new one. Soon after Moultan's wife, Abigail, died, and he immediately married her scandalously younger best friend. And, undoubtedly in the mind to save money, recycled his first wife's wedding ring by giving it to his new bride.

The night of their wedding Abigail's ghost is said to have appeared to the newlywed couple, demanding her jewelry back. No one seems to know if the rings were returned or how long the couple was plagued by the unhappy ghost of Moultan's first wife, but the younger woman must have loved him. She stayed with him, ghosts and all, until he died in 1787. In a final twist on the unusual life of Jonathan Moultan, pall bearers at his funeral dropped the casket. When the lid sprung open everyone gathered saw not the body of a man in his seventies, but a box of gold coins with the devils face stamped on them.

How much of these stories are true, and how much has been invented over the course of time is debatable, but Jonathan Moultan was in fact buried without a tombstone and the site of his grave is not only unmarked, but unknown. Moultan now has a memorial stone that was put up in his honor, but no body is buried there. He is the only high-ranking Revolutionary War hero in New Hampshire whose grave site is unknown. Which is definitely an unusual ending for a wealthy businessman and close friend of George Washington.

Moultan's house, the one legend says is built with bricks burnt by the anger of the Devil, is still standing and has been privately owned since the turn of the twentieth century. It has always been the most famous of Hampton's haunted houses. Servants in the home have reported seeing ghosts in its stately hallways since Moulton's time. One family who owned the home after Moultan's death had an exorcism performed there but the ghost stories have still persisted.

Mysterious Lights

In 1998, for several days in March, multiple witnesses called in reports of strange lights hovering over the ocean near Hampton Beach. Many of these witnesses got photographs and video of the green lights which were described as emanating from a tadpole shaped aircraft of some kind.

Some witnesses also said that later on in the evening, after witnessing the lights, they had splitting migraine headaches and a series of nightmares. The headaches and bad dreams seemed to crop up again each evening that the lights returned. When the lights stopped appearing over the ocean, the headaches and nightmares also left, never to return.

A year later, in North Hampton, a man awoke when a bright light shone through the skylight in his bedroom. The light was a tight intense beam that was so carefully controlled that whomever was directing it was able to point it from a great distance directly into the man's right eye.

When the man went to sit up the beam of light retracted and he had a brief glimpse of something large, oval shaped and bright speeding away through the trees.

New Castle

New Castle is the state of New Hampshire's smallest town, ironically located on what is nicknamed "The Great Island." It is home to both Fort Constitution and the Portsmouth Harbor Lighthouse, which can be confusing since those attractions are generally considered to be firmly those of the city of Portsmouth even though they are located in the island that is home to the village of New Castle.

The Oldest True Ghost Story

Joseph Citro, a folklorist and author of such books as Weird New England and Cursed in New England: Stories of Damned Yankees, tracked down a well-documented case of possible poltergeist activity that happened in New Hampshire all the way back in 1682. The story takes place in New Castle and, if Joseph Citro's research is correct, it holds the current title as the oldest known reporting of a true haunting in the United States.

In 1682, New Castle was just as small, if not smaller, than it is today and there was no way the Walton family could keep the extraordinary things happening to them a secret for very long. One terrible morning, the family woke up to hear a strange sound from outside. It sounded, vaguely, like rain but much, much heavier. Running outside they realized the frightening truth. The house wasn't getting rained on, the house was being pelted with stones!

Some as small as pebbles, others large enough to leave a good-sized bruise if they struck you, the flurry of rocks appeared to be falling directly out of the sky. What made this freakish weather phenomena even more unusual was that the storm of stones was directed solely at the Walton homestead; the rest of New Castle was enjoying a warm spring day, without a cloud in the sky. Neighbors were soon drawn by the noise, and everyone searched in vain trying to find the source of the outburst.

Odder still, when the Waltons went back inside their home to get away from the sharp sting of rocks, they discovered that it was raining rocks inside, as well as out. The floor of the house was already covered in several inches of rock. The family knew the stones couldn't be coming through the windows, as they were all closed and locked.

The Walton's continued to be plagued by falling rock for some months. There seemed to be no way for anyone in the family to get away from it. When they fled the house and took up residence with a friend, the stones followed them. When they gave up and moved back into the house, the rocks ceased falling at their friends home. Not only could no one imagine how the rocks had gotten there, they couldn't figure out where anyone would get so many stones to begin with.

At one point, the head of the Walton household, George Walton himself, gathered up some of the stones after a particularly heavy rainfall, marked them with paint, and locked them away in the house. Within a few days the stones had removed themselves from where they were hidden and once again rained down on the Walton home. George saw the painted-on stones fall back out of the sky with his own two eyes.

As you can imagine, the weather problems that followed the family were big news back in 1682, just as much as they would be today. The family was very well thought of in town, and the notion of them trying to pull off such an elaborate hoax was unthinkable. On top of their outstanding reputations, much of the Walton family troubles were witnessed by Richard Chamberlain, who was secretary of the colony of New Hampshire at the time. He was an adamant supporter of the family, and the authenticity of the bizarre occurrences happening to them. With such a prestigious witness on scene, it was not long before scientists came from all over the country, and all over the world, to either find a rational explanation for the problem or to debunk the Waltons outright. Every last one of them would leave confused and angry when one after another of their experiments failed to produce results. The scientists could not come up with even one theory that the rocks didn't defy. The fall of rocks was, and remains to be, a mystery.

After some time, the rain of stones stopped, and didn't start again. Eventually, an old woman who was a neighbor of the Walton's would be accused of using witchcraft against the family. The woman was, perhaps, lucky in the fact that the events at the Walton household occurred ten years before the witch-hunting craze struck in Salem, or she may have met with a terrible fate for the townspeople's suspicions against her.

Wentworth by the Sea Resort Hotel and Spa

It is ironic to think that the tiny town of New Castle is home to such an enormous hotel as the Wentworth by the Sea. It is even funnier to think that as huge as the Wentworth is today, it is only a fraction of the size it was during most of its nearly hundred and thirty year-long history.

Considering the import of pubs and breweries in old Portsmouth, it should come as no surprise that the massive Wentworth by the Sea Hotel was started by a distiller. Daniel Chase, originally of Somerville, Massachusetts, built an eighty-two room resort named Wentworth Hall. Several owners, and several name changes later, it passed hands to another brewery owner, Frank Jones. Frank Jones added an another floor onto the hotel bringing the grand total of rooms up over 300. Jones also built a sailboat launch, a clubhouse, a golf course, an icehouse, and expanded the hotels gardens.

Over the years, the Wentworth was visited by movie stars, royalty, presidents, artists, and writers. It hosted the 1905 negotiations between Russian and Japan that ended the Russo-Japanese War. These talks would win President Theodore Roosevelt a Nobel Peace Prize.

By the mid 1980s, though it seemed the Wentworth's heyday was over, large sections of the hotel had been torn down or left to gather dust. It was bought, sold, and bought again several times over. Local citizens, concerned over the decay of such an important historical landmark, tried to save the hotel but with its size and seaside location, it came at a high price. In 1999, the closed hotel was used as a set in the horror movie In Dreams, starring Annette Benning and Robert Downey, Jr. It was not re-opened as a hotel until 2003.

Today, the Wentworth by the Sea Resort Hotel and Spa is owned by Marriott Hotels and the company put a great deal of effort into restoring the old hotel to its former glory. It is a premier travel destination with more than 10,000 square feet of meeting and conference space, 116 rooms, an outdoor pool, and a 6,300 square-foot day spa. The entire space has been thoroughly modernized and decorated in high Victorian fashion. It is a little slice of yesterday with all the service and all the amenities you would expect from a five-star hotel.

The Wentworth by the Sea is so glamorous and beloved that more than a few ghosts have stayed on to enjoy everything it has to offer. Late at night, you can sometimes hear lively party music from the 1920s playing on the ocean breeze and sometimes you can even catch of glimpse of the party goers as they walk around the beautifully landscaped gardens of the Wentworth. These party goers have been spotted dressed in the trendiest fashions of several long-gone eras. The ghosts of the Wentworth come from so many different time periods, and the hotel has changed, grown, and shrunk so much over the years, that they are often seen passing right through walls and other structures.

Rye

Rye was dubbed one of the 20 best places in the world to retire to by Barron's Magazine, and its beach area has been described as the "Gold Coast" of New England. It is an upscale New England beach town that attracts tourists along with more than a few ghosts.

The Ghost of Goldie

It is ironic, considering Rye's "Gold Coast" moniker, that the ghost who haunts the restaurant called Ray's Seafood is named Goldie. Goldie haunts the top floor of the restaurant and is most known for unlocking doors and opening windows.

One suspects that whoever Goldie is, she must have been a mother. One night, some underage workers decided to help themselves to a few drinks after closing. Before they could even take a sip, the phone started to ring incessantly. When they answered it, no one was there, but as soon as they hung up, the ringing started again. When the

People expect to find ghosts in buildings that are hundreds of years old. They usually don't expect to find them at their favorite ocean front seafood place.

strange events with the phone didn't stop them, the glasses in the bar started to shake uncontrollably, even though no one else in the neighborhood felt any Earthquake-like tremors. The only explanation anyone could think of was that Goldie wanted to keep the kids from doing something they shouldn't.

The Farragut Hotel

The Philbrick's were a hotel family long before New Hampshire's seacoast was anything resembling a tourist attraction. The jewel of their hotels was the Atlantic House, which was built by Ephraim Philbrick and opened in Rye in the early 1800s. By 1846, the hotel had passed into the hands of Ephraim's son, John, and, for reasons lost to history, the Atlantic House was moved directly across the street from its original location.

This "new" Atlantic House was a popular spot for locals and hosted a variety of entertainment in the summers. Each year saw more and more additions being added to the already large and opulent hotel. Many celebrities and politicians passed through its doorways in the 1800s, and in 1866, David Farragut was a guest of the hotel. David Farragut was an admiral in the Navy during the Civil War who, in the Battle of Mobile Bay, famously exclaimed "Damn the torpedoes, full speed ahead!"

At this point, much impressed by their guest and wanting to advertise his stay there, the Philbrick's changed the name of the hotel to the Farragut Hotel. After the name change, the hotel had a tumultuous history. It was burned to the ground, rebuilt, added to, torn down, and passed through the hands of the Philbrick family and into the hands of Harry Beckwith, who owned the slightly more famous and opulent Wentworth Hotel. Beckwith had no better luck than the Philbricks did. The Farragut Hotel closed in 1974 and was demolished a year later. Then, a year after that another "new" Farragut Hotel was built on the site, but the inside was never completed. Currently, the well maintained, though still simply an exterior shell, version of the new-new Farragut Hotel is owned by the DeMoula family who own, of course, the DeMoula's and Market Basket grocery store chains. The family has had a long standing feud that has made its way into court at least once, and the Farragut Hotel has lain vacant because of it.

The unfinished shell of the hotel, and the fourteen acres of land it belongs to, are worth an estimated 1.7 million dollars. Representatives say that there is no plan for the hotel to be finished, or opened, and that it is most definitely not up for sale.

The hotel being unfinished hasn't seemed to made one bit of difference to the ghosts that haunt the site. Two ghosts are well known to people in the area and there may be many more just waiting to make their presence known. One ghost seems drawn to the area of the old gift shop, the other has musical inclinations and can be heard, though never seen. Many people have reported hearing ghostly piano music drifting up from the empty ground where the Farragut Hotel's theater once stood.

The Arbor Inn

Between the ski country in the northern part of the state and the resort towns of the seacoast, New Hampshire boasts many world-class accommodations for travelers. The Arbor Inn certainly heads up that list. It has won awards for everything from its Inn to its pancakes, both locally and at the national level. Most guests simply have a nice stay at a gorgeous inn, but every so often, a guest gets a ghostly encounter along with their delicious pancake breakfast.

The Inn's owners prefer to be known for their customer service rather than their ghosts, so the experiences people have had at the Arbor Inn are not as well publicized as you find at many of the Portsmouth area hotels. It seems to be a fairly low-level haunting that only people with an already-existing sensitivity pick up on. Guests have mentioned missing items, that mysteriously pop back up when they politely ask the thin air around them to give the item back, and light switches that turn themselves on and off at will.

Strange noises, like footsteps, are sometimes mentioned and a few people have even heard their name being called out in otherwise empty rooms which suggests that the ghosts at The Arbor Inn are aware of their surroundings and happy to have a little attention every now and again.

The Brackett Massacre

Sandy Beach, located in Rye, has an unhappy history of its own. In the late 1600s, it was the site of the Brackett Massacre. While farmers plowed their fields, close to forty Native American's came down from York, Maine, and descended on the quiet community. Several of the townsfolk were killed and an unknown number of women and children were kidnapped and brought to Canada. Bernice Remick was one of these kidnapped girls and when she was older, she left Canada and came back to Sandy Beach to reclaim her family's lands. This property later passed into the hands of the Rye Conservation Commission and is now open to the public.

People visiting Sandy Beach in September, particularly around the anniversary of the Brackett Massacre, sometimes get a very unique look at the history of this place. They have reported hearing unearthly screams and the sounds of a fierce battle they cannot see. A few visitors have claimed to have seen figures that look like they are engaged in an eternal battle.

Sandy Beach is not the only place where the spectral remains of massacre victims can be found in Rye. Little Harbor was also the location of a seventeenth-century massacre where fourteen farmers lost their lives. Like Sandy Beach, the spirits of both the villagers and the Native Americans who fought them for the land, are sometimes sensed by people who come to this spot.

Despite historic markers such as this one few people know about the Brackett Massacre that occurred in New Hampshire. The spirits of those who were killed serve as a much more remarkable remembrance of the tragedy.

Odiorne Point State Park

Located right near Little Harbor is Odiorne Point State Park. Odiorne Point State Park is one of the most haunted places in New England—if not the entire country. Odiorne Point State Park is an excellent spot to look for the several ghost ships that sail New Hampshire's coast. From its banks you have a clear view of the path that two of the Isles of Shoals famous ghost ships are known to sail.

The park is also home to Olde Odiorne Point Cemetery, a place that many historians speculate is the oldest cemetery in New Hampshire, as well as being one of its best kept secrets. Despite how well maintained it is, and the many stones dating from the seventeenth and eighteenth centuries, you won't find Olde Ordiorne Point Cemetery in the usual guidebooks. Perhaps because of how quiet it is around Olde Odiorne Point Cemetery, it seems to have become a haven for ghosts. Voices are the most commonly reported occurrence here, oftentimes by people who happen upon the cemetery by chance. More than a few people said they were even drawn to the spot because of the voices. As you walk between the tombstones, many worn down to plain nubs of rock, you hear voices calling out names and dates. Maybe the spirits are trying to get visitors to remember who they are, now that time has erased the names and dates of birth and death from their gravestones.

Within Odiorne Point State Park itself visitors often get a much more up close and personal experience from its ghosts. There is one spirit that likes to follow people as they hike the trails at the park. Most hikers describe it simply as feeling as though they are not alone on the wooded path they are following, a distinct feeling of being followed, or of eyes watching them. A few hikers have even heard footsteps behind them, but when they turn around, they find nothing there. One hiker heard the footsteps behind him for several long minutes and when he turned around to confront the stalker, not only did he see no person, but the footsteps quickened their pace—running right at him! Even though the hiker couldn't see his pursuer, he braced himself for the jolt as the running footsteps neared. All he was hit with was a cloud of cold dense air that left him shivering and scared.

Despite this unusual encounter, overall, the ghostly hiker seems to be a benign presence in the park. One woman said that when she was hiking at Odiorne Point State Park on her own one afternoon, she got a little turned around and couldn't remember how to get back to where she had parked her car. Before she could begin to really worry, she felt an unseen hand grip hers and gently lead her towards the right path. Within a few minutes, she recognized where she was, realized she was only a few minutes from her vehicle, and the feeling of being held by the hand disappeared.

World War II Spirits

Odiorne Point State Park has some more unusual ghosts as far as New England hauntings go. Where the park now stands, there were once close to a dozen summer homes. These homes, and the lands surrounding them, were seized by the Government at the beginning of World War II. The homes, including a twenty-four bedroom estate and a rather famous seaside resort, were torn down so the land could be used to defend Portsmouth Harbor and the Portsmouth Naval Shipyard. The land was torn up and huge guns, capable of firing 138-pound shells up to fifteen miles away, military bunkers, and underwater listening devices were installed. Ironically, none of these items were ever used and by the time they were constructed, most of them were already terribly obsolete.

But that does not mean that the construction had no impact on Odiorne Point State Park. Today, you can still walk the grounds once owned by the United States Government and see the remains of the "Panama" mounts the guns would have been attached to and see the large hillocks created by the underground bunkers. This site has had a less tangible presence as well. The bunkers are located at a paranormal hotspot where visitors sometimes hear gunfire, yelling, screams, and even cries of victory. Psychics visiting the area explain that the site seems to be a haven for spirits of the men who died in World War II, even if they didn't die at Odiorne Point State Park.

Orb Photography

The most common ghostly experience that visitors to Odiorne Point State Park report is that of orb photography. Orbs are the usually small gray-ish to green-ish to yellow-ish fuzzy spheres that sometimes show up in photographs. Skeptics pass them off as dust on the lens while others say they prove ghostly emanations. No matter what your explanation is, for whatever reason, photographs of Odiorne Point State Park not only seem to be more likely to have orbs in them, but you are also more likely to get pictures of these orbs in multitudes. Pictures showing dozens upon dozens, if not hundreds upon hundreds, or variously colored orbs are taken here quite often.

Afterward

I have many writer friends who have always tell me that "once you make it big time, you won't have to do all those events anymore!" I think that they are trying to be reassuring. I find it to be anything but. I love doing events and I have been lucky enough to be invited to give many speeches, interviews, readings, and book signings. I love talking to readers and I love all the stories I hear from them while I am out and about promoting my books. Most people come to my readings armed with photographs of the old family barn where there is a shape that might, or might not, be the spirit they believe slams the door on windless nights. Or with a tape recording they accidentally made in an empty room where several chattering voices can just barely be heard through the static. I always joke that after doing an event, I could write an entire new book just of the stories readers have come to tell me.

Of course, not all readers come with a story to tell. Many come armed with questions. Questions about ghosts, about writing, and about anything paranormal. They want to know how long it took me to write my books (my least favorite question), if I live in a haunted house myself (I hope not), if I have ever seen a ghost (maybe . . .), do I watch Ghosthunters and Paranormal State (I have seen some episodes, but I don't watch the shows religiously), how do ghosts fit into the idea of heaven and hell (your local priest is better equipped to answer that question than I) and for advice on how they can get published themselves (write, submit, repeat).

But the thing I probably get asked most often is, "Do you believe in ghosts?" The answer to that question is yes, no, and maybe. I don't have an easy answer to that one, which perplexes a lot of people who have read my books. I get the general feeling from people that they want their ghostly authors to believe in the things that go bump in the night wholeheartedly. No reservations allowed. And when I answer they usually walk away with a look on their face that clearly says I have confused and disappointed them. If they have already shared their own haunted experience with me, sometimes the look on their face borders on betrayal and I think, if they could, they would snatch that story right out of my head and take it back.

I know that I believe in something, and if ghost is the term people want to attach to it, well that's fine by me. I hear so many different people tell me about similar unexplainable experiences they all have in the same place and I hear so many stories with the same elements from people from all over in all different places. While researching these books, attending signings, and giving readings, I hear time and time again:

"I lived in a haunted house . . ."
"My house is haunted . . ."
"This one time the strangest thing happened . . ."

I refuse to believe that all these people are imagining the same thing. I refuse to believe that all of these people are playing a prank or looking for attention, which is sometimes said (not by me!). Every day we learn more, and science explains more, so who is to say that the unexplained experiences these people have had will never be explained someday?

I learned early on in writing ghost books to bring a friend with me when I take pictures. While researching and writing Manchester Ghosts I entered and left Valley Street Cemetery a total of five different times before giving up and asking my husband to come with me. But, for me at least, it's hard to know when I'm experiencing something real and when I'm letting my imagination run away with me! And yes, many times while visiting these haunted places I ended up with what paranormal investigators call "orb" photos, those funny, fuzzy, glowing colored dots that sometimes appear on a printed photograph even though they weren't on scene at the time. But I'm not well versed enough in photography to tell you if I simply had some dust on my camera lens or if I captured some kind of proof of life after death.

I think most people are like me, they are an "open-minded skeptic" as one reporter called me. For some people, the stories in this book are glimpses of a possible afterlife, evidence of people living on after death. For others they are simply entertainment, something a little spooky, fun but not real. Or they read it as an interesting look into the history of Portsmouth that you don't normally hear about, and that's fine, too. I think that these ghost stories are important, whether they are real, or legends, or myth or whatever, because they are our modern folklore. Many of the stories are quite old and have been told since our grandparents' time, some are modern.

. . .And who knows if, someday, our grandchildren will be hearing a version of these very stories as they sit around the campfire?

Bibliography

Blackman, W. Haden. *The Field Guide to North American Hauntings: Everything You Need to Know About Encountering Over 100 Ghosts, Phantoms, and Spectral Entities.* New York, New York: Three Rivers Press, 1998.

D'Agostino, Thomas. *Haunted New Hampshire.* Atglen, Pennsylvania: Schiffer Books, 2007.

D'Entremont, Jeremy. "Boon Island Light." Lighthouse.cc.

Drake, Samuel. "New England Legends and Folk Lore. " Secaucus, New Jersey: Castle Books, 1993.

Fabrizio, Richard. "South Cemetery: Peaceful Present, not so restful past." *Portsmouth Herald*, November 4, 2001. Portsmouth, New Hampshire.

Feals, Jennifer. "Exposure: Jeremy D'Entremont, Lighthouse Enthusiast." Seacoastonline.com.

Filgate, Michelle. "Portsmouth Ghost Stories." *Main Street Magazine.*

Gore, Moody P. and Guy E. Speare. "New Hampshire Folk Tales." Plymouth, New Hampshire, 1932.

Gosling, Nick. "Ghosts, Murderers, and Beer." WireNH.com, October 26, 2005.

Granato, Sherri. "Haunted America: Portsmouth, New Hampshire" Associated Content. April 10, 2007.

Gray, T.M. "Ghosts of Maine." Atglen, Pennsylvania: Schiffer Books. 2008.

Johnson, Chloe. "UFOs: Is Seeing Believing? A Retired UNH Professor Says the Truth is Out There." The Citizen of Laconia. February 24, 2008.

Johnson, Scott A. "The Isles of Shoals." HorrorChannel.com

Jones, Eric. "New England Curiosities: *Quirky Characters, Roadside Oddities and Other Offbeat Stuff.* Globe Pequot Press. 2006, Guilford, Connecticut.

Keene, Pamela and Melanie, with Auger Kevin. "Lady Ghost, Rockingham Hotel & John Paul Jones: Ghost, Lost Love, Haunted House." SeacoastNH.com.

Morse, Susan "Rye's 22-year-old, Unfinished Farragut Hotel Receives Face-lift." July 28, 1998. SeacostOnline.com.

Ogden, Tom. "The Complete Idiots Guide to Ghosts and Hauntings." United States: Alpha Books, 1999.

Pecci, Alexandra. "Award-winning Pancakes and Ghostly Guests." *The Eagle Tribune*. March 16, 2008.

Robinson, J. Dennis. "As I Please: The Truth about Ocean Born Mary." SeacoastNH.com

Robinson, J. Dennis. "Misty Legends of Sam Haley." SeacoastNH.com.

Rogak, Lisa. "Stones and Bones of New England: A Guide to unusual, Historic, and otherwise Notable Cemeteries." *The Globe Pequot Press*. 2004, Guildford, Connecticut.

Rondina, Christopher. "The Vampire Hunters Guide to New England: True Tales of the Yankee Undead." North Attleboro, Massachusetts: Covered Bridge Press, 2000.

Rutledge, Lyman V. "Ten Miles Out: Guidebook to the Isles of Shoals, Portsmouth, New Hampshire" Portsmouth, New Hampshire: Peter E. Randall, 1997.

Sharp, David. "For lease: Naval Prison—Used, Needs TLC." *The San Francisco Chronicle*. May 18, 2008.

Southall, Richard. *How to be a Ghost Hunter.* Saint Paul, Minnesota: Llewellyn Publications, 2003.

Zwicker, Roxie. *Haunted Portsmouth: Spirits and Shadows of the Past.* Haunted America, a division of The History Press, 2007. United Kingdom.

Web Site Resources

The following Web sites were instrumental in the researching of Ghosts of Portsmouth, New Hampshire:

Angelsghosts.com
AssociatedContent.com
CowHampshire.com
Ghosts.org
GraveMatter.com
Hampton.Lib.Nh.us
HauntedHouses.com
HollowHill.com
HorrorChannel.com
Lighthouse.cc
NewEnglandCuriosities.com
NewHampshire.com
NHMufon.com
ParanormalNewEngland.tripod.com
PortsmouthNH.com
RyeReflections.org
SeacoatNH.com
Smuttynose.com
StrawberyBanke.org
TheShadowLands.net
Wikipedia.org

Index